HSPT Test Prep

HSPT Test Prep

Three Full-Length Tests with Detailed
Answer Explanations

ANTHEM PRESS

Anthem Press
An imprint of Wimbledon Publishing Company
www.anthempress.com

This edition first published in UK and USA 2023
by ANTHEM PRESS
75–76 Blackfriars Road, London SE1 8HA, UK
or PO Box 9779, London SW19 7ZG, UK
and
244 Madison Ave #116, New York, NY 10016, USA

British Library Cataloguing-in-Publication Data
A catalogue record for this book is available from the British Library.

Library of Congress Control Number: 2023931923
A catalog record for this book has been requested.

ISBN-13: 978-1-83998-902-5 (Pbk)
ISBN-10: 1-83998-902-5 (Pbk)

This title is also available as an e-book.

Contents

Introduction

High School Placement Test (HSPT Exam) is a high school entrance exam taken by students in grade 8 seeking admission to parochial high schools. The HSPT is a five-section, multiple-choice standardized exam. The test is published by Scholastic Testing Service.

It is a five-part, 298-question test. Students are given 2 hours and 21 minutes to complete the exam. It is divided into five sections: Verbal Skills, Quantitative Skills, Reading Comprehension & Vocabulary, Mathematics Concepts, and Language Skills.

Summary

Who can take the test?	Students from grade 8
When is the test conducted?	Every year on the **first Friday of November**
What is the format of the test?	All questions are multiple choice
What is the medium of the test?	Paper based
What are the topics covered in the test?	Verbal Skills Quantitative Skills Reading Comprehension & Vocabulary Mathematics Concepts Language Skills
How long is the test?	Total test duration is **2 hours 21 minutes and contains 298 questions** distributed as below: Verbal Skills: 60 questions; 16 minutes Quantitative Skills: 52 questions; 30 minutes Reading Comprehension & Vocabulary: 62 questions; 25 minutes Mathematics Concepts: 64 questions; 45 minutes Language Skills: 60 questions; 25 minutes

High School
Placement Test 1

Verbal Skills

You have 16 minutes to answer the 60 questions in the Verbal Section.

> ## Directions:
> Choose the best answer for each question.

1. Which among the words below is synonymous with novice?

   (A) Expert   (B) Master   (C) Beginner   (D) Experienced

2. Which among the words below does not belong with the others?

   (A) Sandra   (B) Emily   (C) Elsa   (D) Girl

3. Matchstick is to ignite as extinguisher is to

   (A) Light   (B) Burn   (C) Spoil   (D) Douse

4. Which among the words below does not belong with the others?

   (A) Spoon   (B) Salt   (C) Sugar   (D) Soy sauce

5. Joy is to gleeful as melancholy is to

   (A) Proud   (B) Gloomy   (C) Amused   (D) Cheerful

6. Alex gets paid more than Mark. Will gets paid more than Alex. Mark gets paid more than Will. If the first two statements are true, this means that the third sentence is

   (A) False   (B) True   (C) Unknown

7. Which among the words below closely mean the same with <u>emulate</u>?

   (A) Oppose   (B) Ignore   (C) Imitate   (D) Contradict

8. Which among the words below does not belong with the others?

   (A) Superficial   (B) Deep   (C) External   (D) Outer

9. Person is to councillor as place is to

   (A) Noun   (B) Street   (C) Common   (D) Subject

10. Which among the words below closely means to <u>disgust</u>?

    (A) Admiration (B) Respect (C) Accept (D) Despise

11. Toni is the younger brother of Mike. Mike is the older brother of Lily. Lily is the youngest among the siblings. If the first two statements are true, then the third statement is

    (A) True (B) False (C) Uncertain

12. Frugal is the new black. Frugal in the first sentence is a/an

    (A) Noun (B) Adjective (C) Verb (D) Adverb

13. A snake is a cold-blooded animal. It is a/an

    (A) Reptile (B) Mammal (C) Animal (D) Pet

14. Sand is to desert as tree is to

    (A) Ocean (B) Forest (C) Sky (D) Space

15. Senator is to politics as teacher is to

    (A) Classroom (B) School (C) Education (D) Faculty

16. Which among the words below does not belong with the others?

    (A) Inescapable (B) Inevitable (C) Unavoidable (D) Fate

17. Spontaneous is synonymous with

    (A) Calculated (B) Planned (C) Conscious (D) Impulsive

18. To slack is to fail as to study is to

    (A) Decline (B) Diminish (C) Pass (D) Decay

19. The speaker came five minutes after the schedule. He is

    (A) Early (B) Late (C) Intelligent (D) Tall

20. Eric leaves the house earlier than Rose. Belle leaves the house earlier than Eric. Rose leaves the house later than Belle. If the first two statements are true, then the third statement is

    (A) True (B) False (C) Uncertain

21. Michelle is to she as Ralph is to

    (A) He (B) His (C) Him (D) It

22. Which among the words below does not belong with the others?

(A) Ears (B) Eyes (C) Nose (D) Cheeks

23. Subtle is synonymous with

(A) Obvious (B) Understated (C) Beautiful (D) Wise

24. Christmas came early. Early in the first statement is a/an

(A) Adjective (B) Verb (C) Adverb (D) Pronoun

25. The early bird catches the worm. Early in the first statement is a/an

(A) Adverb (B) Noun (C) Adjective (D) Verb

26. Road is to car as railway is to

(A) Train (B) Boat (C) Bus (D) Truck

27. Mozambique has lowest annual rainfall trends recorded. The land is

(A) Fertile (B) Wet (C) Green (D) Arid

28. Image is to pretty as character is to

(A) Villain (B) Humble (C) Slim (D) Protagonist

29. Preacher is to church as supervisor is to

(A) Team (B) Class (C) Role (D) Leadership

30. Which among the words below does not belong with the others?

(A) Coach: sports (B) Teacher: education (C) Secretary: manager (D) Manager: business

31. Square is to triangle as circle is to

(A) Shape (B) Circumference (C) Round (D) Semicircle

32. Roses are more expensive than lilacs. Orchids are more expensive than roses. Lilacs are cheaper than orchids. If the second and third statements are true, then the first statement is

(A) True (B) Uncertain (C) False

33. Amicable is synonymous with

(A) Friendly (B) Hostile (C) Dangerous (D) Troublesome

34. Human is to mundane as superhero is to

(A) Boring (B) Ordinary (C) Supernatural (D) Routine

35. Window is to house as cable is to

(A) Long (B) Bridge (C) Connect (D) City

36. Purple is to blue as orange is to

(A) Red (B) Yellow (C) White (D) Brown

37. Which among the words below does not belong with the others?

(A) She (B) He (C) You (D) His

38. Paul threw the ball to Sam to catch. <u>Catch</u> in the first statement is a/an

(A) Verb (B) Noun (C) Adjective (D) Adverb

39. Paul thought Sam was a good catch. <u>Catch</u> in the first statement is a/an

(A) Verb (B) Noun (C) Adjective (D) Adverb

40. Procrastinate is synonymous with

(A) Ready (B) Early (C) Delay (D) Fast

41. Spin is to dizzy as jump is to

(A) Play (B) Fall (C) Elevate (D) Skip

42. Which among the words does not belong with the others?

(A) Pen (B) Notebook (C) Pencil (D) Marker

43. Hear is to here as dear is to

(A) Loved one (B) Adjective (C) Dare (D) Deer

44. Brick is to road as glass is to

(A) Bottle (B) Water (C) Wine (D) Hard

45. Diligent is to industrious as humorous is to

(A) Boring (B) Funny (C) Intelligent (D) Practical

46. Love is to hate as remember is to

(A) Think   (B) Dream   (C) Forget   (D) Note

47. Which among the words below does not belong with the others?

(A) Consider: review   (B) Troubled: calm   (C) Keep: trash   (D) Walk: run

48. Which among the words below does not belong with the others?

(A) Yellow   (B) Blue   (C) Red   (D) Green

49. Which among the words below does not belong with the others?

(A) Blue green   (B) Green   (C) Violet   (D) Orange

50. Which among the words below does not belong with the others?

(A) Orange: fruit   (B) Blue: color   (C) Happiness: joy   (D) Love: action

51. Which best describes the word <u>accentuate</u>?

(A) Elongate the stress   (B) Prolong the intonation   (C) Make more noticeable

(D) Mask the obvious

52. Which best describes the word <u>analogy</u>?

(A) Synonymous   (B) Comparison   (C) Part   (D) Example

53. Which best describes the word <u>obscure</u>?

(A) Obvious   (B) Known   (C) Prominent   (D) Uncertain

54. Which word is synonymous with the word <u>expedite</u>?

(A) Accelerate   (B) Delay   (C) Late   (D) Hinder

55. Which word is synonymous with the word <u>coalition</u>?

(A) Argument   (B) Debate   (C) Alliance   (D) Dispute

56. Which of the words below does not belong with the others?

(A) Skip: skipped   (B) Think: thought   (C) Speak: spoke   (D) Has: have

57. Which of the words below does not belong with the others?

(A) Most   (B) Anyone   (C) Everyone   (D) Someone

58. Which word is synonymous with underpin?

    (A) Abandon   (B) Defend   (C) Fight   (D) Negate

59. Which word is synonymous with restrain?

    (A) Allow   (B) Control   (C) Permit   (D) Push

60. Doll is to toy as phone is to

    (A) Model   (B) Expensive   (C) Gadget   (D) Network

End of section.

If you have any time left, go over the questions in this section only.

Do not start the next section.

You have 30 minutes to answer the 52 questions in the Quantitative Skills Section.

Directions:

Choose one answer—the answer you think is best—for each problem.

---

61. What is 4 more than 25% of 40?

(A) 11   (B) 19   (C) 16   (D) 14

62. Look at this series 42, 46, 50, 54 … . What number should come next?

(A) 58   (B) 57   (C) 60   (D) 56

63. Look at this series 48, 51, 56, 63, … . What number should come next?

(A) 72   (B) 75   (C) 70   (D) 67

64. Examine (P), (Q), and (R) and find the best answer.

(P)   (Q)   (R)

(A) (P) plus (Q) is less than (R)   (B) (R) is equal to (P)   (C) (Q) is greater than (P)

(D) (P) is greater than (Q) and (R) both

65. Examine (P), (Q), and (R) and find the best answer.

(P) 0.925   (Q) $\frac{5}{7}$ (R) 0.93 × 2.4

(A) (P) is less than (R) but greater than (Q)   (B) (R) is the smallest

(C) (P) plus (Q) is greater than (R)   (D) (Q) plus (R) is greater than (P)

66. What number is the cube of 6 divided by 3?

    (A) 84   (B) 72   (C) 96   (D) 108

67. What number is $\frac{1}{4}$ of the average of 12, 19, 7, 14, and 8?

    (A) 60   (B) 12   (C) 6   (D) 3

68. Examine (P), (Q), and (R) and find the best answer.

    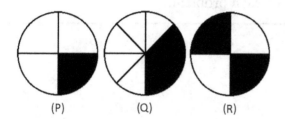

    (P)   (Q)   (R)

    (A) (P) is the larger   (B) (R) is the greatest   (C) (P) plus (Q) is less than (R)

    (D) 2 time of (P) is equal to (Q)

69. Look at the series 1, 3, 7, 9, 13, ... What number should be filled next in the series?

    (A) 15   (B) 17   (C) 19   (D) 16

70. Examine (P), (Q), and (R) and find the best answer.

    (P) 20% of 90   (Q) 90% of 20   (R) 14% of 300

    (A) (P) plus (Q) is greater than (R)   (B) (P), (Q), and (R) are equal   (C) (P) is greater than (R)

    (D) (R) is greater than (P)

71. Look at the series 1, 3, 6, 8, 16, 20, ... What number should come next?

    (A) 22   (B) 32   (C) 40   (D) 24

72. What will be 3 less, 9% of 900?

    (A) 81   (B) 90   (C) 78   (D) 99

73. What number is square of 12 divided by 6?

    (A) 144   (B) 24   (C) 72   (D) 108

74. What number is 7 less than $\frac{1}{4}$ of 32?

    (A) 8   (B) 15   (C) 1   (D) 0

75. What will be the value of this operation?

$4 \times (24 - 9) \div 5$

(A) 45   (B) 12   (C) 4   (D) 120

76. Look at the series 794, 785, 778, 773, ... What number should come next?

(A) 767   (B) 763   (C) 770   (D) 761

77. Look at the series 96, 99, 102, ____, 108, 111. What number should fill the blank in the middle of the series?

(A) 104   (B) 107   (C) 105   (D) 106

78. What number divided by 6 is $\frac{1}{4}$ of 20?

(A) 5   (B) 6   (C) 30   (D) 24

79. What number multiplied by 4 is 7 less than 19?

(A) 12   (B) 7   (C) 3   (D) 4

80. What number divided by 4, leaves 8 more than 12?

(A) 20   (B) 40   (C) 60   (D) 80

81. Examine (P), (Q), and (R) and find the best answer if both x and y are greater than zero.

(P) 2x + 2y   (Q) 5x + 2y   (R) 3x

(A) (P) plus (Q) is greater than (R)   (B) (P) is the larger

(C) (P) plus (R) is equal to (Q)   (D) (Q) is less than (R)

82. Look at the series and find the next number: 7, 14, 15, 30, ...

(A) 60   (B) 33   (C) 35   (D) 31

83. What number subtraction from 5 leaves $\frac{1}{3}$ of 24?

(A) 8   (B) 3   (C) 24   (D) 13

84. $\frac{1}{3}$ of what number is 7 times 2?

(A) 42   (B) 14   (C) 21   (D) 6

85. What is 2 greater than $\frac{4}{5}$ of 10?

    (A) 8 (B) 10 (C) 2 (D) 6

86. Examine the graph and find the best answer.

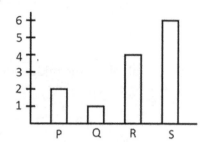

    (A) P plus Q is less than R (B) Q is the largest (C) S is the smallest

    (D) R plus Q is greater than S

87. Look at the series and find the next number: 2, 4, 3, 9, 4, 16, 5, ...

    (A) 6 (B) 25 (C) 10 (D) 32

88. What number is 4 times $\frac{1}{4}$ of 20?

    (A) 5 (B) 20 (C) 10 (D) 16

89. What number is 20 more than $\frac{5}{9}$ of 27?

    (A) 15 (B) 20 (C) 47 (D) 35

90. What number is 9 more than 4 squared?

    (A) 27 (B) 7 (C) 25 (D) 13

91. Look at the series: 10, 16, 32, 38, 76, ____. What will be the next number?

    (A) 76 (B) 144 (C) 78 (D) 82

92. $\frac{1}{4}$ of what number added to 7 is equal to 2 times 6?

    (A) 5 (B) 12 (C) 20 (D) 19

93. Two non-perpendicular and non-parallel lines are called _____

    (A) Normal lines (B) Tangent lines (C) Oblique lines (D) None of these

94. What is 5% of 250?

(A) $12\frac{1}{2}$ (B) 10   (C) 5   (D) None of these

95. Which shape has three sides?

(A) Square   (B) Circle   (C) Triangle   (D) Pentagon

96. What is the cube root of 1728?

(A) 8   (B) 12   (C) 16   (D) 14

97. {A, B, C} – {B} =

(A) {A,B, C}   (B) {A,B}   (C) {A, C}   (D) {A}

98. Find the tenth digit from this number 1729.0429

(A) 2   (B) 0   (C) 9   (D) 1

99. Write as a decimal $\frac{4}{5}$, is

(A) 0.75   (B) 0.80   (C) 0.90   (D) 0.40

100. The measure of $\angle A$ is

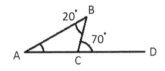

(A) $\angle A = 90°$ (B) $\angle A = 110°$ (C) $\angle A = 50°$ (D) $\angle A = 130°$

101. {P, E, N} ∪ {P, E, N, C, I, L}

(A) {P, E, N}   (B) {P, E }   (C) {P, E, N, C, I, L}   (D) { C, I, L}

102. Simplify $4(-4)^2$

(A) –64   (B) 16   (C) –16   (D) 64

103. Which of the following is the pair of reciprocals?

(A) (4, –4)   (B) $\left(\frac{12}{7}, \frac{7}{12}\right)$ (C) (1, –1)   (D) $(4^3, 3^4)$

104. The circumference of this circle is

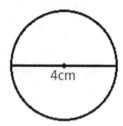

4cm

(A) 8π cm   (B) 4π cm   (C) 16π cm   (D) 2π cm

105. The ratio of 50¢ and $1.70 is

(A) $5:17$ (B) $5:8$ (C) $5:8.5$ (D) $8.5:17$

106. How many natural numbers are between 0 and 1

(A) 2   (B) 0   (C) Uncountable   (D) 1

107. Find the ratio between 5 days and 1 week

(A) $5:1$ (B) $5:7$ (C) $5:6$ (D) $1:5$

108. The ratio between 2 yards to 18 inch is

(A) $1:9$ (B) $4:1$ (C) $9:1$ (D) $1:4$

109. Which of the following is true?

(A) $(b+c) \div a = \dfrac{a}{b} + \dfrac{a}{c}$ (B) $ax + bx + c = a(x + b + c)$ (C) $X^2 + ax = x(X + a)$

(D) $\dfrac{a}{x} + b = \dfrac{a+b}{x}$

110. The square root of 205 is between

(A) 15 to 16   (B) 14 to 16   (C) 90 to 100   (D) 17 to 18

111. Which one of the following is true?

(A) $10 \le 1.0$ (B) $-12 \le -15$ (C) $0.01 < 0.20$ (D) $17 > 20$

112. ΔABC and ΔMBN are similar triangle. Then find the length of MN

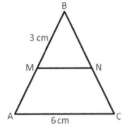

(A) MN = 3 cm   (B) MN = 2 cm   (C) MN = 6 cm   (D) None of these

End of section.

If you have any time left, go over the questions in this section only.

Do not start the next section.

You have 25 minutes to answer the 62 questions in the Reading Comprehension and Vocabulary Sections.

Directions:
Read each passage carefully and choose the best answer for each question.

According to the theory of the scientist Charles Darwin (1809–1882), humans evolved from primates around ten to twelve million years ago which split into two lineages and evolved separately and then became the variety of species known to man today. The evolution happened through natural selection. Natural selection is the result of increased reproductive capacities that are best suited for the conditions which the organisms are living. His theory was the organisms evolved as a result of many tiny changes over the course of time.

113. Who theorized the evolution?

    (A) Charles Darwin (B) Primates (C) Scientists (D) Organisms

114. According to the theory of evolution, how did the organisms evolve?

    (A) Ten to twelve million years ago (B) Two lineages (C) Natural selection (D) Change

115. Which of the following sentences are true from the passage above?

    (A) Charles Darwin invented the primates (B) Evolution happened ten to twelve million years ago

    (C) There are only two species known to man today (D) The humans evolved from crustaceans

116. What prompted the evolution of organisms according to Charles Darwin?

    (A) Passing time from ten to twelve million years ago (B) The split of two lineages

    (C) Charles Darwin (D) Tiny changes over the course of time

117. How long did Charles Darwin live?

    (A) Unknown (B) Seventy-three years (C) Ten to twelve million years (D) Not long enough

118. According to the passage, when was the theory of evolution invented by Charles Darwin?

    (A) Not stated (B) Yesterday (C) Ten to twelve million years ago (D) 1809

119. The word variety as used and underlined in the passage means

    (A) Uniform (B) One (C) Range (D) Unity

120. The word <u>suited</u> as used and underlined in the passage means

(A) Ill-fitting (B) Loose (C) Contrast (D) Complement

121. What is the complete subject in the last sentence of the passage?

(A) The organisms evolved (B) Evolved as a result of many tiny changes (C) His theory

(D) Over the course of time

122. What is the complete predicate in the last sentence of the passage?

(A) Was the organisms evolved as a result of many tiny changes over the course of time

(B) His theory was the organisms evolved

(C) The organisms evolved as a result of many tiny changes over the course of time

(D) Organisms evolved as a result of many tiny changes over the course of time

Tattoo

What once was meant to be a statement—
a <u>dripping</u> dagger held in the fist
of a <u>shuddering</u> heart—is now just a bruise
on a bony old shoulder, the spot
where <u>vanity</u> once punched him hard
and the ache <u>lingered</u> on. He looks like
someone you had to <u>reckon</u> with,
strong as a stallion, fast and <u>ornery</u>,
but on this chilly morning, as he walks
between the tables at a yard sale
with the sleeves of his tight black T-shirt
rolled up to show us who he was,
he is only another old man, picking up
broken tools and putting them back,
his heart gone soft and blue with stories.

from *Delights & Shadows*, Copper Canyon Press, Port Townsend, WA 2004

123. What does the word <u>dripping</u> as used in the poem means?

(A) Dry (B) Wet (C) Scorched (D) Melting

124. The passage "held in the fist of a <u>shuddering</u> heart" closely means?

(A) Held in the hands of someone who is furious or horrified

(B) Held in the hands of someone who is downhearted

(C) Held in the hands of someone who is jubilant

(D) Held in the hands of someone who is triumphant

125. The underlined word from the passage "the spot where <u>vanity</u> once punched him hard" closely means?

(A) Self-worship   (B) A dressing table   (C) Unfulfilled dreams or goals   (D) Pretension

126. What does the word <u>linger</u> mean?

(A) Walked out   (B) Disappeared quickly   (C) Stayed longer than necessary   (D) Vanished

127. Which of the interpretations below closely relate to the poem?

(A) The man is old enough to have a tattoo   (B) The man's tattoo was poorly done   (C) The poem talked about the old man's lost love as described on the design of his tattoo, which was once his glory, but is just any other man; physical appearance does not define your soul   (D) The man was very old

128. What does the word <u>reckon</u> mean?

(A) Disqualify   (B) Regard   (C) Ignore   (D) Overpower

129. What does <u>ornery</u> mean?

(A) Stubborn   (B) Kind   (C) Honest   (D) Compassionate

130. The passage "heart gone soft and blue" closely means?

(A) The heart has shown gentleness   (B) The heart is tough as stone

(C) The heart has become numb   (D) The heart is sad

A cliff is a mass of rock that rises very high and is almost vertical, or straight up-and-down. Cliffs are very common landscape features. They can form near the ocean (sea cliffs), high in mountains, or as the walls of canyons and valleys. Waterfalls tumble over cliffs. Cliffs are usually formed because of processes called erosion and weathering. Weathering happens when natural events, like wind or rain, break up pieces of rock. In coastal areas, strong winds and powerful waves break off soft or grainy rocks from harder rocks. The harder rocks are left as cliffs. The tiny pieces of rocks broken off by weathering are called sediment or alluvium. Erosion is the process of transportation of this sediment. On sea cliffs, sediment becomes part of the seafloor and is washed away with the waves. On inland cliffs, sediment is often carried away by rivers or winds. Larger rocks broken off by sediment are called scree or talus. Scree builds up at the bottom of many inland cliffs as rocks tumble down. These piles are called scree slopes or talus piles. Some scree slopes can be so large that soil and sediment can build up between the rocks, allowing trees and other vegetation to grow on the slope. Most scientists and mountaineers think the Rupal Flank of Nanga Parbat, a mountain in the Himalayas, is the highest cliff in the world. The Rupal Flank rises 4,600 meters (15,092 feet) above its base. Others say the highest cliff in the world is the east face of Great Trango, in the Karakoram mountain range, which is 1,340 meters (4,396 feet) tall and one of the most difficult rock-climbs in the world. Both Nanga Parbat and Great Trango are located in Pakistan.

131. How does a cliff form?

(A) By the rotation of the earth   (B) Through weathering and erosion   (C) By the gravity of the sun

(D) Unknown causes

132. Which of the following closely means to weathering as described in the article?

    (A) The movement of the planet around its axis   (B) The movement of the planet around the sun

    (C) Breaking up of rocks into sediments by natural causes such as wind or rain

    (D) The gravitational pull of the moon that controls tides

133. Which of the following closely means to erosion as described in the article?

    (A) The formation of boulders due to build up   (B) The breaking up of sediments

    (C) The movement of the broken-up sediment from one place to another

    (D) The formation of volcanoes

134. Which among the sentence below is not true according to the article?

    (A) Cliffs are only formed high in mountains and valleys   (B) Cliffs can be formed near the ocean

    (C) Cliffs can be formed high in mountains   (D) Cliffs can be formed as the walls of valleys

135. What is the meaning of sediment?

    (A) Gaseous substance in the air   (B) Vapor from the bodies of water   (C) Large rocks on a quarry site

    (D) Tiny fragments of rocks that settled at the bottom of a body of water

136. Weathering happens when natural events, like wind or rain, break up pieces of rock. What part of speech is the underlined word as used in the article?

    (A) Verb   (B) Adverb   (C) Noun   (D) Adjective

137. What is another term for sediment as discussed in the article?

    (A) Alluvium   (B) Stone   (C) Particles   (D) Mud

138. Scree builds up at the bottom of many inland cliffs as rocks tumble down. What part of speech is the underlined word as used in the article?

    (A) Rise   (B) Fall   (C) Elevate   (D) Lift

I stood upon a high place, by Stephen Crane

I stood upon a high place,
And saw, below, many devils
Running, leaping,
and carousing in sin.
One looked up, grinning,
And said, "Comrade! Brother!"

139. Which word best describes leaping as used in the poem?

(A) Walk slowly   (B) High jump   (C) Casually pass by   (D) Sprint

140. Which word is synonymous with carousing?

(A) Stay put   (B) Sit idly   (C) Nosily enjoy   (D) Doze off

141. What emotion does the one had when he called the speaker, "Comrade! Brother!"?

(A) Genuine   (B) Having a good time   (C) Disappointed   (D) Sorry

142. Which among the choices below closely interprets the meaning of the poem?

(A) The irony of the speaker looking down on those who he/she thinks are inferior to him

(B) That it is fun to have a good time and not give a care   (C) That drinking and having fun are sins

(D) That the speaker was looking at his brother

Introduction to Poetry
by BILLY COLLINS

I ask them to take a poem
and hold it up to the light
like a color slide

or press an ear against its hive.

I say drop a mouse into a poem
and watch him probe his way out,

or walk inside the poem's room
and feel the walls for a light switch.

I want them to waterski
across the surface of a poem
waving at the author's name on the shore.

But all they want to do
is tie the poem to a chair with rope
and torture a confession out of it.

They begin beating it with a hose
to find out what it really means.

143. "I say drop a mouse into a poem and watch him <u>probe</u> his way out." What does the underlined word as used in the poem mean?

(A) Avoid   (B) Omit   (C) Explore   (D) Reject

144. What figure of speech is used on the line, "and hold it up to the light like a color slide"?

(A) Metaphor   (B) Personification   (C) Simile   (D) Hyperbole

145. What figure of speech is used on the line, "inside the poem's room"?

(A) Metaphor   (B) Personification   (C) Simile   (D) Hyperbole

146. "I want them to waterski <u>across</u> the surface of a poem." What part of speech is the underlined word?

(A) Verb   (B) Noun   (C) Adverb   (D) Preposition

147. Which of the words below is a synonym for the underlined word from question 146?

(A) In   (B) On   (C) Below   (D) Over

148. Which of the interpretations below closely mean to the message of the poem?

(A) This is a message of the author that to understand a poem one must enjoy   (B) The poem is playing with the reader's imagination   (C) The poem is suggesting that we dig our heads into the lines of the poem to understand the meaning   (D) Can't say

First Fig
—Edna St. Vincent Millay

My candle burns at both ends;
It will not last the night;
But ah, my foes, and oh, my friends—
It gives a lovely light!

149. "My candle burns at both ends." What does this line from the poem mean?

(A) She needs a new candle   (B) Her life is fast paced   (C) She lighted both ends of the candle

(D) Can't say

150. Which word closely means to foe?

(A) Comrade   (B) Enemy   (C) Friend   (D) Pal

151. "<u>It</u> gives a lovely light!" What is the preposition "it" from the sentence refer to?

(A) Night   (B) Foes   (C) Candle   (D) Friends

152. Which is the best interpretation of the poem?

(A) The author is living in a fast lane trying to finish multiple things at a time   (B) The author is ready to sleep as her candle burns   (C) The author does not have power supply which is why she must burn her candle at both ends   (D) Can't say

Vocabulary

Directions:
Choose the word that closely means the same as the underlined word.

153. Lacking in <u>empathy</u> to prioritize his own need

    (A) Distance from the other person   (B) Disperse into groups   (C) Cut means of communication

    (D) Understand and share the feelings of others

154. Monochromatic for an <u>aesthetic</u> appeal

    (A) Unappealing   (B) Pleasing   (C) Disgust   (D) Eerie

155. True <u>camaraderie</u> wins championships

    (A) Solidarity   (B) Solitude   (C) Lonesome   (D) Competitive

156. His <u>impetuous</u> decision to elope

    (A) Thought of   (B) Impulsive   (C) Long awaited   (D) Careful

157. Wore the diamond ring <u>ostentatiously</u>

    (A) Humbly   (B) Shyly   (C) Showy   (D) Hidden

158. To be <u>resilient</u> during this challenging times

    (A) Recover quickly   (B) Lose hope   (C) Get stuck   (D) Give up

159. A <u>reclusive</u> cabin in the middle of nowhere

    (A) Crowded   (B) Narrow   (C) Towering   (D) Secluded

160. <u>Parched</u> from the summer heat

    (A) Well fed   (B) Drunk   (C) Full   (D) Thirsty

161. As his <u>transient</u> popularity took a dive

    (A) Long term   (B) Short lived   (C) Permanent   (D) Constant

162. Took the child to the town's <u>venerable</u> healer

    (A) Dishonorable   (B) Disreputable   (C) Honorable   (D) Unknown

163. Be <u>wary</u> of passersby in the dark

(A) Cautious   (B) Trustful   (C) Unwary   (D) Inattentive

164. Like an <u>ephemeral</u> gone in a minute

(A) Long lasting   (B) Year round   (C) Brief   (D) Eternal

165. Survive war and escape <u>tyranny</u>

(A) Peace   (B) Cruelty   (C) Friendship   (D) Freedom

166. <u>Vengeance</u> for those fallen victim of inequality

(A) Kindness   (B) Forgiveness shown toward someone whom it is within one's power to punish or harm   (C) Punishment inflicted or retribution exacted for an injury or wrong   (D) Readiness to show appreciation for and to return kindness

167. <u>Immensely</u> satisfying to the heart

(A) Extremely large or great, especially in scale or degree   (B) Extremely or unusually small   (C) Restricted in size, amount, or extent   (D) On one occasion or for one time only

168. Stress from financial <u>liabilities</u>

(A) A useful or valuable thing, person, or quality   (B) Accountability   (C) An abundance of valuable possessions or money   (D) Freedom from disturbance

169. The <u>monotony</u> of the countryside

(A) Tedious repetition and routine   (B) Absence of uniformity, sameness   (C) Assortment

(D) Variety

170. <u>Sensible</u> things to spend your hard-earned money on

(A) Not fulfilling   (B) Not expected to achieve the intended purpose   (C) Impractical   (D) Practical and functional rather than decorative

171. <u>Eschew</u> evil

(A) Avoid   (B) Close   (C) Stick   (D) Follow

172. His injury <u>precluding</u> a spot in the sports league

(A) Despite   (B) Including   (C) Excluding   (D) Along with

173. As the children <u>deplored</u> the loss of their class pet rabbit

(A) Cheer   (B) Grief   (C) Celebrate   (D) Award

174. The deafening <u>tumult</u> at the town square

    (A) Noisy commotion   (B) Silence   (C) Serenity   (D) Solitude

End of section.

If you have any time left, go over the questions in this section only.

Do not start the next section.

Mathematics Concepts

You have 45 minutes to answer the 64 questions in the Mathematics Concepts Section.

Directions:

Choose one answer—the answer you think is best—for each problem. You may use scratch paper when working on these problems.

---

175. The prime factorization of 20 is

(A) 2.2.5   (B) 2.10   (C) 5.4   (D) 1.20

176. {S, O, F, T, W, A, R, E} ∩ {H, D, W, A, R, E} is equal to

(A) {φ}   (B) {S, O, F, T, H, D, W, A, R, E}   (C) {W, A, R, E}   (D) None of these

177. Which one of the properties is associative property?

(A) P.(r.q) = (p.r).q   (B) P.q = q.r   (C) P.1 = p   (D) P.0 = 0

178. Solve: $16 - 4\frac{3}{4} =$

(A) $12\frac{1}{4}$ (B) $11\frac{1}{4}$ (C) $10\frac{1}{4}$ (D) $19\frac{1}{4}$

179. Mr. Smith paid $624.96 for electric bills last year. How much he paid in one month average?

(A) 53.30   (B) 52.03   (C) 51.4   (D) 55.70

180. Solve: 7 + (−4) + 6 + (−9)

(A) 10   (B) −10   (C) −7   (D) 7

181. If the 5% sales tax on a computer was $80, what was the price of the computer without the tax?

(A) $1,600   (B) $1,420   (C) $1,520   (D) $1,620

182. Solve: $3\frac{1}{6} + 2\frac{4}{6}$

(A) $4\frac{5}{6}$ (B) $5\frac{4}{6}$ (C) $5\frac{5}{12}$ (D) $5\frac{5}{6}$

183. If $-7 + 8x = 25$, $x =$

(A) 3   (B) 2   (C) 4   (D) 5

184. Mr. Adam paid $40 interest on a loan that had a 5% simple interest rate. How much money did he borrow?

(A) $975   (B) $351   (C) $800   (D) $850

185. If a flagpole has a shadow 42 feet long when 7-feet man's shadow is 14 feet long. What is the height of the flag?

(A) 21 feet   (B) 14 feet   (C) 28 feet   (D) None of these

186. If A = 5, B = 3, then 4A + 2B =

(A) 22   (B) 8   (C) 26   (D) 24

187. $5(6x - 2) = 20$, $x =$

(A) 4   (B) 3   (C) 2   (D) 1

188. Four years ago, Jones's father was 4 times as old as Jones. How old is Jones's father now if Jones is 14?

(A) 10   (B) 18   (C) 40   (D) 44

189. Solve $2\frac{4}{3} - 1\frac{2}{3}$

(A) $1\frac{2}{3}$ (B) $2\frac{2}{3}$ (C) $\frac{2}{3}$ (D) $1\frac{4}{3}$

190. What will 8 ft. by 12 ft. rectangular rug cost at $4 a square yard?

(A) $96   (B) $384   (C) $284   (D) $484

191. The ratio of $\frac{4}{5}$ and $\frac{9}{10}$

(A) 8 to 9   (B) 9 to 10   (C) 10 to 8   (D) 9 to 8

192. Solve $\frac{3.9276}{7.21}$

(A) 0.503   (B) 5.03   (C) 0.0503   (D) 0.53

193. What is the volume of the solid where height = 12 cm, length = 8 cm, breath = 4 cm.

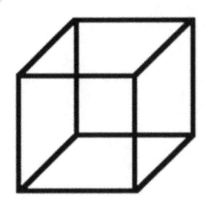

(A) 324 cc   (B) 384 cc   (C) 834 cc   (D) 483 cc

194. If A = 4, B = 6, C = 5, then $\dfrac{2BC}{A}$ = ?

(A) 30   (B) 15   (C) 20   (D) 25

195. If $\dfrac{4x}{5}$ = 32 then x =

(A) 5   (B) 8   (C) 23   (D) 40

196. Solve 62.19 × 0.0763

(A) 4.724808   (B) 4.742804   (C) 4.7442808   (D) 4.742808

197. 2.70, 2.75, 2.80, 2.85, 2.90, ... What number should come next in this sequence?

(A) 2.95   (B) 2.90   (C) 3.00   (D) None of these

198. Solve $4x - 9 = 7x - 33$, then x =

(A) 24   (B) 8   (C) 7   (D) 9

199. If A% of 50 is 12, A =

(A) 12%   (B) 20%   (C) 24%   (D) 34%

200. The greatest common factor of 14, 28 is

(A) 2   (B) 17   (C) 14   (D) 28

201. Solve 72,592 × 190

(A) 17,392,480   (B) 19,732,480   (C) 147,921,380   (D) 13,792,480

202. The product of 5 and 6 is 3 more than P. What is P?

(A) 33   (B) 30   (C) 27   (D) None of these

203. Solve $9 \times 2 \div (4 \times 3)$

(A) 9   (B) $\dfrac{9}{2}$ (C) $\dfrac{3}{2}$ (D) None of these

204. If ab + 27 = 55 and a = 7, b =

(A) 28   (B) 7   (C) 4   (D) 27

205. Find the area of the triangle whose dimensions are h = 24 inch, b = 12 inch.

(A) 288 sq. inch   (B) 72 sq. inch   (C) 144 sq. inch   (D) None of these

206. $\dfrac{7x}{4} + 2 = 30$, then $x =$

(A) 4   (B) 28   (C) 16   (D) 7

207. Solve, $x^2 + 7 = 88$.

(A) ± 7   (B) ± 6   (C) ± 9   (D) ± 8

208. Find the surface area of the cube whose base a = 6 cm.

(A) 36 cm²   (B) 216 cm²   (C) 256 cm²   (D) 324 cm²

209. Find the $\angle ACD$

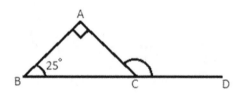

(A) 25°   (B) 115°   (C) 75°   (D) 65°

210. Solve $42 \div \dfrac{1}{6}$

(A) 6   (B) 7   (C) 36   (D) 67

211. What is 3 more than 40% of 100

(A) 37   (B) 47   (C) 43   (D) 33

212. Solve $x : 3x + 4 > 2x + 7$

(A) $x > 7$ (B) $x > 3$ (C) $x < 3$ (D) $x = 3$

213. Solve x : 4.5x + 13.5 = 54

(A) 40.5   (B) 40   (C) 9   (D) 8

214. Solve 0.702 + 4.9 + 5.14 =

(A) 10.472   (B) 12.707   (C) 10.472   (D) 10.742

215. $\sqrt{x^2 + 25} = 13$ then $x =$

(A) 8   (B) 144   (C) 12   (D) 5

216. r = 42 − (2 × 7)(n) where n = 2, r =

(A) 16   (B) 28   (C) 61   (D) 22

217. A square has an area of 64 sq. in. The value of the perimeter is

(A) 8   (B) 16   (C) 24   (D) 32

218. $(7 + 8)^2 =$

(A) 225   (B) 125   (C) 522   (D) 252

219. Find the circumference of the circle whose diameter 12 cm

(A) 6π cm   (B) 36π cm   (C) 12π cm   (D) 18π cm

220. Increased by 120%, the number 80 becomes

(A) 82   (B) 120   (C) 84   (D) 92

221. 2x + 3y = 11, x + y = 3 then y =

(A) −1   (B) −5   (C) 84   (D) 92

222. Jenny left her home for school at 7:50 a.m., and she come back after school at 1:40 p.m. How long was she not in her home?

(A) 6 Hrs. 50 mins   (B) 4 Hrs. 50 mins   (C) 5 Hrs. 40 mins   (D) 5 Hrs. 50 mins

223. Solve for x in the following equation:
2.5x + 6 = 13.5

(A) 2.5   (B) 3.5   (C) 4.5   (D) 6.5

224. 24 more than a certain number is 58. What is the number?

(A) 72   (B) 25   (C) 24   (D) 23

225. 40% of what number is equal to 12?

    (A) 40   (B) 30   (C) 20   (D) 50

226. If 9x – 3y = 3, and x = 1, what does y equal?

    (A) 2   (B) 3   (C) 4   (D) 1

227. $s = t(8 + 5) - (11 - t)$ and t = 1; what does s equal?

    (A) 2   (B) 3   (C) 4   (D) 1

228. $15^2 =$

    (A) 144   (B) 169   (C) 196   (D) 225

229. $(15 \times 7) + 12 =$

    (A) 105   (B) 111   (C) 117   (D) 128

230. 300% of 90 =

    (A) 90   (B) 180   (C) 270   (D) 360

231. Which of the following number sentence is true?

    (A) 5 feet > 4 feet   (B) 8 feet < 6 feet   (C) 2 feet > 6 feet   (D) 4 feet < 2 feet

232. Look at this series: 3, 7, 11, 15, … . What number should come next?

    (A) 17   (B) 18   (C) 19   (D) 20

233. $(9 - 3)^4 =$

    (A) 36   (B) 216   (C) 1296   (D) 512

234. What is the value of y when x = 4 and y = 7 + 8x?

    (A) 24   (B) 37   (C) 27   (D) 31

235. Find the circumference of the circle whose diameter is 8 cm

    (A) 4π cm   (B) 12π cm   (C) 8π cm   (D) 16π cm

236. The square root of 309 is between

    (A) 15 to 16   (B) 16 to 17   (C) 90 to 100   (D) 17 to 18

237. Solve x : 5x + 7 > 3x + 11

(A) x > 2   (B) x > 3   (C) x < 2   (D) x = 2

238. What number is the average of 16, 13, 4, 14, and 8?

(A) 55   (B) 5   (C) 11   (D) 45

End of section.

If you have any time left, go over the questions in this section only.

Do not start the next section.

You have 25 minutes to answer the 60 questions in the Language Section.

Directions:

Look for errors in capitalization, punctuation, or usage. Choose the answer with the errors. If no errors found, choose D.

239. (A) The brown Fox jumped over the fence.
     (B) The little chick cried for help.
     (C) He said, "I will be leaving soon."
     (D) No mistake

240. (A) Is there anything you can't do?
     (B) The amount of patience I have put on you is unimaginable.
     (C) Its their time to face the press.
     (D) No mistake

241. (A) Their is no greater pleasure than seeing your children succeed in life.
     (B) The constitution was established long before I was born.
     (C) Anna wanted to tell you to stay at home.
     (D) No mistake

242. (A) Sports is an enjoyable topic to discuss.
     (B) One-half of the class is here.
     (C) Everyone votes for Karen as president.
     (D) No mistake

243. (A) What?
     (B) How did this happen!
     (C) Please, stop.
     (D) No mistake

244. (A) I placed the book in the top of the table.
     (B) Where are you at?
     (C) I can see your true colors behind that mask.
     (D) No mistake

245. (A) I must tell Will how I feel.
    (B) She just cant take her hands off the trophy.
    (C) Its skin has turned brown.
    (D) No mistake

246. (A) The United States have been every emigrant's dream.
    (B) Helping is rewarding task.
    (C) When you see them coming, run!
    (D) No mistake

247. (A) Honoring your parents is one of the Ten Commandments.
    (B) Chances are, you're going to the same university.
    (C) Your in my spot!
    (D) No mistake

248. (A) Let's go to the beach!
    (B) What is taking so long?
    (C) Where have you been?
    (D) No mistake

Directions:

Identify which part of speech is the underlined word.

249. Katherine jumped <u>over</u> the fence to sneak into the party.

    (A) Noun (B) Preposition (C) Adverb (D) Adjective

250. I like <u>running</u>.

    (A) Noun (B) Verb (C) Adverb (D) Preposition

251. There are <u>many</u> options to choose from.

    (A) Noun (B) Verb (C) Adjective (D) Adverb

252. He took the same bus <u>by chance</u> and saw the love of his life.

    (A) Noun (B) Verb (C) Adjective (D) Adverb

253. <u>Her</u> job was to call potential buyers so she can make a sale.

    (A) Noun (B) Pronoun (C) Verb (D) Adjective

254. The bus continues <u>to</u> the South.

(A) Noun   (B) Preposition   (C) Adverb   (D) Adjective

255. <u>As</u> I say my prayer, I remember how good my day was.

(A) Noun   (B) Verb   (C) Conjunction   (D) Preposition

256. I <u>quickly</u> closed my eyes as I heard footsteps behind the door.

(A) Adjective   (B) Adverb   (C) Verb   (D) Noun

257. Waiting <u>for</u> you was the best decision I have ever made.

(A) Adjective   (B) Preposition   (C) Noun   (D) Adverb

258. There were snakes crawling <u>about</u> in the grass

(A) Preposition   (B) Noun   (C) Adverb   (D) Adjective

259. I was <u>unable</u> to get out of the crowd.

(A) Noun   (B) Pronoun   (C) Adjective   (D) Adverb

260. The weather will be good <u>this weekend</u> according to Tom.

(A) Noun   (B) Adverb   (C) Pronoun   (D) Adjective

Directions:

Identify which sentence is grammatically correct and follows the correct sentence structure.

---

261. (A) Alexa shared, "there is no doubt that the culprit is among us."
(B) Alexa shared "there is no doubt that the culprit is among us."
(C) Alexa shared "There is no doubt that the culprit is among us."
(D) Alexa shared, "There is no doubt that the culprit is among us."

262. (A) Either the policemen or the chief catches a break from crime.
(B) Either the policemen or the chief catch a break from crime.
(C) Neither the policemen or the chief catches a break from crime.
(D) Neither the policemen nor the chief catches a break from crime.

263. (A) The plan is set.
(B) An plan is set.
(C) The Plan is set.
(D) An Plan is set.

264. (A) Half of the committee has voted him out.
(B) Half of the committee have voted him out.
(C) Half of the committee is voted him out.
(D) Half of the committee will voted him out.

265. (A) Half of the committee is not satisfied with his leadership.
(B) Half of the committee are not satisfied with his leadership.
(C) Half of the committee has not satisfied with his leadership.
(D) Half of the committee have not satisfied with his leadership.

266. (A) Two-thirds of the pizza were eaten by Jacob.
(B) Twenty percent of the answers was wrong.
(C) Seventy-five percent of the casts are biracial.
(D) Three-fourths of the trees has been cut down.

267. (A) My dad's collection of books are as diverse as the one's from a public library.
(B) My dad's collection of books were as diverse as the one's from a public library.
(C) My dad's collection of books is as diverse as the one's from a public library.
(D) None of the above

268. (A) Breaking and entering have been common in the neighborhood lately.
(B) Breaking and entering has been common in the neighborhood lately.
(C) Breaking and entering are common in the neighborhood lately.
(D) Breaking and entering will be common in the neighborhood lately.

269. (A) Three miles is too far to travel on foot.
(B) Three miles is too far to travel on foot.
(C) Three miles have been too far to travel on foot.
(D) Three miles will too far to travel on foot.

270. (A) Five dollars has fallen from the bag.
(B) Five dollars have fallen from the bag.
(C) Five dollars will fallen from the bag.
(D) Five dollars were fallen from the bag.

271. (A) If Sheila were here, she'd totally sing this song.
(B) If Sheila was here, she'd totally sing this song.
(C) If Sheila can be here, she'd totally sing this song.
(D) If Sheila will be here, she'd totally sing this song.

272. (A) When Mike and Will arrives, they find that their friends have started ordering from the menu.
(B) When Mike and Will arrive, they find that their friends has started ordering from the menu.
(C) When Mike and Will arrive, they find that their friends have started ordering from the menu.
(D) None of the above

273. (A) Unless our student council members really come in early, We will not finish the meeting on time.
(B) Unless our student council members really comes in early, we will not finish the meeting on time.
(C) Unless our student council members really came in early, we will not finish the meeting on time.
(D) Unless our student council members really come in early, we will not finish the meeting on time.

274. (A) Kate, of all the applicants who is applying for the job, is the best.
(B) Kate, of all the applicants who are applying for the job, is the best.
(C) Kate, of all the applicants who are applying for the job, are the best.
(D) None of the above

275. (A) Carmen's dogs, which are kept by the yard, bark all day long.
(B) Carmen's dogs, which is kept by the yard, bark all day long.
(C) Carmen's dogs, which are kept by the yard, barks all day long.
(D) None of the above

276. (A) In the end, they lives happily ever after.
(B) In the end, They will lived happily ever after.
(C) In the end they lived happily ever after.
(D) In the end, they lived happily ever after.

277. (A) When coach Paul say practice at 5 a.m., he means 4:30 a.m.
(B) When coach Paul says practice at 5 a.m., he means 4:30 a.m.
(C) When Coach Paul says practice at 5 a.m., he means 4:30 a.m.
(D) None of the above

278. (A) I am enrolled in health Aide as part of the health science program at University of Health Sciences.
(B) I am enrolled in Health Aide as part of the Health science program at University of Health Sciences.
(C) I am enrolled in Health Aide as part of the health science program at University of Health Sciences.
(D) None of the above

Spelling

Directions:

Identify which among the words is spelled incorrectly. If nothing is misspelled, write N on your answer sheet.

279. (A) Communicable
     (B) Commission
     (C) Iliteracy
     (D) Literature

280. (A) Baeutiful
     (B) Queue
     (C) Tongue
     (D) Gouge

281. (A) Cooperration
     (B) Irrigation
     (C) Mitigation
     (D) Corruption

282. (A) Illicit
     (B) Mallet
     (C) Bullet
     (D) Filet

283. (A) Gregariously
     (B) Canoeing
     (C) Frugivoruos
     (D) Serviceable

284. (A) Flocculent
     (B) Inccessantly
     (C) Effervescence
     (D) Cataclysmic

285. (A) Innuendeos
     (B) Chaos
     (C) Focus
     (D) Tornados

286. (A) Exhumation
     (B) Erosion
     (C) Adhesion
     (D) Attension

287. (A) Vicereine
     (B) Caffeine
     (C) Bulletein
     (D) Certain

288. (A) Evidentary
     (B) Parliamentary
     (C) Unnecessary
     (D) Penitentiary

Sentence Composition

Directions:

Choose the best words to complete the sentences.

289. Global warming a never-ending conversation throughout the globe.

     (A) Was (B) Is (C) Had (D) Will

290. The chance given to restore faith taken for granted.

     (A) Is (B) Will be (C) Has been (D) Was

291. The oceans have been crying for help a long time.

     (A) For (B) At (C) To (D) On

292. Our children be the one to suffer in the future.

     (A) Is (B) Should (C) Are (D) Will

293. There will be a time the air we breathe becomes a cost we cannot afford.

   (A) When   (B) For   (C) Because   (D) It

294. Now the time and everything we do moving forward will still matter.

   (A) Are   (B) Has   (C) Is   (D) Will

295. Among the participants, the guest's speech on financial literacy the most awaited.

   (A) Were   (B) Was   (C) Will   (D) Have

296. Neither Anne nor her relatives seen the news.

   (A) Is   (B) Are   (C) Has   (D) Have

297. Neither Anne's relatives nor she seen the news.

   (A) Is   (B) Are   (C) Has   (D) Have

298. A stary car jumped the counter (direction: down from the counter as the start point)

   (A) Off   (B) On   (C) At   (D) Above

End of section.
If you have any time left, go over the questions in this section only.

ANSWER KEY

1. C	31. D	61. D	91. D	121. C	151. C	181. C	211. C	241. A	271. A
2. D	32. B	62. A	92. C	122. A	152. A	182. D	212. B	242. D	272. C
3. D	33. A	63. A	93. C	123. B	153. D	183. C	213. C	243. D	273. D
4. A	34. C	64. C	94. A	124. A	154. B	184. C	214. A	244. A	274. B
5. B	35. B	65. A	95. C	125. C	155. A	185. A	215. C	245. B	275. A
6. A	36. B	66. B	96. B	126. C	156. B	186. C	216. A	246. A	276. D
7. C	37. D	67. D	97. C	127. D	157. C	187. D	217. D	247. C	277. B
8. B	38. A	68. B	98. B	128. B	158. A	188. D	218. A	248. D	278. C
9. B	39. B	69. A	99. B	129. A	159. D	189. A	219. C	249. B	279. C
10. D	40. C	70. D	100. C	130. A	160. D	190. B	220. D	250. A	280. A
11. C	41. C	71. A	101. C	131. B	161. B	191. A	221. D	251. C	281. A
12. A	42. B	72. C	102. D	132. C	162. C	192. A	222. D	252. D	282. N
13. A	43. D	73. B	103. B	133. D	163. A	193. B	223. B	253. A	283. C
14. B	44. A	74. C	104. B	134. A	164. C	194. B	224. C	254. B	284. B
15. C	45. B	75. B	105. A	135. D	165. B	195. D	225. B	255. C	285. A
16. D	46. C	76. C	106. B	136. C	166. C	196. D	226. A	256. B	286. D
17. D	47. A	77. C	107. B	137. A	167. A	197. A	227. B	257. B	287. C
18. C	48. D	78. C	108. B	138. B	168. B	198. B	228. D	258. A	288. A
19. B	49. A	79. C	109. C	139. B	169. A	199. C	229. C	259. C	289. B
20. A	50. C	80. D	110. B	140. C	170. D	200. C	230. C	260. B	290. C
21. A	51. C	81. C	111. C	141. B	171. A	201. C	231. A	261. D	291. A
22. D	52. B	82. D	112. A	142. A	172. C	202. C	232. C	262. D	292. D
23. B	53. D	83. D	113. A	143. C	173. B	203. C	233. C	263. A	293. A
24. C	54. A	84. A	114. C	144. C	174. A	204. C	234. D	264. B	294. C
25. C	55. C	85. D	115. B	145. B	175. A	205. C	235. C	265. A	295. B
26. A	56. D	86. A	116. D	146. D	176. C	206. C	236. D	266. C	296. D
27. D	57. A	87. B	117. B	147. D	177. A	207. C	237. A	267. C	297. C
28. B	58. B	88. B	118. A	148. A	178. B	208. B	238. C	268. B	298. A
29. A	59. B	89. D	119. C	149. B	179. B	209. B	239. A	269. A	
30. C	60. C	90. C	120. D	150. B	180. B	210. B	240. C	270. B	

NOTE: To calculate Raw score, allocate 1 point for each correct answer and 0 points for each incorrect and unanswered questions.

Number of correct answers = _____ (A)

Number of incorrect or unanswered answers = _____ (B)

Final Raw score = A – B = _____ - _____ = _____

EXPLANATIONS

Verbal Skills

1. The correct answer is (C). Novice is a person new to or inexperienced in a field or situation.

2. The correct answer is (D). Sandra, Emily, and Elsa are proper nouns. Letter D is a common noun.

3. The correct answer is (D). This is a sample of a cause—effect relationship. A matchstick can ignite a flame; an extinguisher can douse a flame.

4. The correct answer is (A). Salt, sugar, and soy sauce are condiments. Spoon is a utensil.

5. The correct answer is (B). The first pair of words is a noun—adjective relationship. Gleeful is used to describe someone who feels great joy; gloomy is used to describe someone who feels distressed or down.

6. The correct answer is (A). Will gets paid more than Alex who also gets paid more than Mark; therefore, it is only false that Mark gets paid more than Will.

7. The correct answer is (C). Emulate is to equal or approach equality with.

8. The correct answer is (B). Superficial, external, and outer are all synonyms which is used to describe something existing on the surface. Deep is the antonym of the three adjectives.

9. The correct answer is (B). This is a sample of a general–specific relationship. A councillor is a particular person; street is a particular place.

10. The correct answer is (D). Disdain is the feeling that someone or something is unworthy of one's consideration or respect; contempt. Both disdain and disgust are feelings of disapproval.

11. The correct answer is (C). If the first two statements are true, we cannot be certain that Lily is the youngest among the siblings because she can be older or younger than Toni who is the younger brother of Mike.

12. The correct answer is (A). Frugal is the subject of the sentence which means it is a noun.

13. The correct answer is (A). To support the first statement, a reptile is a cold-blooded vertebrate.

14. The correct answer is (B). This is a sample of a part–whole relationship. Sand makes up a desert; trees make up a forest.

15. The correct answer is (C). A senator is into political activities; a teacher is a steward of education. Politics and Education are both general classifications of different fields.

16. The correct answer is (D). Fate is a noun. The words inescapable, inevitable, and unavoidable are adjectives which can be used to describe someone's fate.

17. The correct answer is (D). The word spontaneous is used to describe an act performed or occurring because of a sudden inner impulse or inclination.

18. The correct answer is (C). This is a sample of a cause–effect relationship. If you slack, you may fail; if you study, you may pass.

19. The correct answer is (B). To support the first statement, someone coming in after the scheduled time is considered late.

20. The correct answer is (A). If Belle leaves the house earlier than Eric, who leaves the house earlier than Rose, then Belle must leave earlier than Rose. Therefore, the third statement is true.

21. The correct answer is (A). The word she is a personal pronoun referring to a female. He is its male counterpart.

22. The correct answer is (D). Eyes, nose, and cheeks are parts of your face. Ears are not on your face but are parts of your head.

23. The correct answer is (B). Subtle means not immediately obvious or comprehensible.

24. The correct answer is (C). The word early in the statement modifies the verb "came," therefore is an adverb.

25. The correct answer is (C). The word early in the statement modifies the noun "bird," therefore is an adjective.

26. The correct answer is (A). This is a sample of a part–whole relationship. Cars take the road; trains take the railway.

27. The correct answer is (D). Arid means having little or no rain.

28. The correct answer is (B). This is a sample of a noun–adjective relationship. The word pretty is an adjective used to describe an image or outer appearance; the word humble is an adjective used to describe character of a person.

29. The correct answer is (A) This is a sample of an object–purpose relationship. The purpose of a preacher is to lead the church; the supervisor leads the team.

30. The correct answer is (C). A, B, and D are person–field relationships. The word pairs are the people and the field of their expertise. C is superior to subordinate relationship. A secretary reports to a manager.

31. The correct answer is (D). This is a sample of a cause–effect relationship. You get a triangle if you diagonally cut a square; you get a semicircle if you cut a circle in half.

32. The correct answer is (B). If the second and third statements are true, it is uncertain that roses are more expensive than lilacs. Roses can be more expensive or cheaper than lilacs. Exhibit A and B below may both be true.

Exhibit A	Exhibit B
Orchids - $3	Orchids - $3
Lilacs - $2	Lilacs - $1
Roses - $1	Roses - $2

33. The correct answer is (A). Amicable means having a spirit of friendliness; without serious disagreement or rancor.

34. The correct answer is (C). This is a sample of a noun–adjective relationship. Mundane means of this earthly world; supernatural means beyond the laws of nature or science.

35. The correct answer is (B). This is a sample of a part–whole relationship. A window is a part of a house; a cable is a part of a bridge.

36. The correct answer is (B). This is a sample of a cause–effect relationship. You get purple when you mix blue with red; orange when you mix yellow with red. Red is the constant variable.

37. The correct answer is (D). A, B, and C are all subjective personal pronouns. The word "his" is the only possessive personal pronoun from the choices.

38. The correct answer is (A). The word <u>catch</u> in the statement is used as an action. It is a verb.

39. The correct answer is (B). <u>Catch</u> in the statement is a noun which refers to Sam.

40. The correct answer is (C). To procrastinate is to delay or postpone action.

41. The correct answer is (C). This is a sample of a cause–effect relationship. When you spin you can get dizzy as an aftermath; when you jump, you get elevated from the ground.

42. The correct answer is (B). Pen, pencil, and marker are tools to write with; a notebook is where you write on.

43. The correct answer is (D). The first pair is a homonym. Deer closely sounds the same as dear.

44. The correct answer is (A). This is a sample of a part–whole relationship. A road is made up of bricks; a bottle is made up of glass.

45. The correct answer is (B). The first pair of words in the sentence is synonyms. Diligent is having or showing care and conscientiousness in one's work or duties which means similar with industrious. Humorous means causing lighthearted laughter and amusement; comic.

46. The correct answer is (C). The word pairs are opposite actions. They are antonyms.

47. The correct answer is (A). The other pairs are opposite actions and are antonyms. The first word pair are synonyms.

48. The correct answer is (D). Yellow, blue, and red are all primary colors. Green is a secondary color which is a result of mixing yellow and blue.

49. The correct answer is (A). Blue green is a tertiary color in the traditional color wheel. The rest are secondary colors.

50. The correct answer is (C). Letter C is a sample of a synonym analogy/relationship. The other pairs are example-type analogies. Orange is a fruit. Blue is a color. Love is a feeling.

51. The correct answer is (C). To accentuate is to make something more noticeable or prominent.

52. The correct answer is (B). Analogy is a comparison between two things, typically for the purpose of explanation or clarification. The comparison can be between any kind of relationship between two things such as synonyms, antonyms, example, part, etc.

53. The correct answer is (D). Obscure means not discovered or known about; uncertain.

54. The correct answer is (A). To expedite is to make (an action or process) happen sooner or be accomplished more quickly.

55. The correct answer is (C). Coalition is a union into one body or mass: fusion.

56. The correct answer is (D). Letter D is a word pair both in present tense; has for singular and have for plural. The other pairs are the base form of the verb and their past tenses.

57. The correct answer is (A). Most is a quantifier and is used for plural nouns. The other words are called singular indefinite pronouns and uses a singular form of verb. An indefinite pronoun does not refer to any specific person, thing, or amount.

58. The correct answer is (B). Underpin is to support, justify, or form the basis for. To underpin is to defend.

59. The correct answer is (B). Restrain means to keep under control or within limits.

60. The correct answer is (C). This is a sample of example-type analogy. A doll is a toy; a phone is a gadget.

Quantitative Skills

61. The correct answer is (D). Start by finding 25% of 40: $0.25 \times 40 = 10$. Then add 4, $10 + 4 = 14$.

62. The correct answer is (A). The pattern in this series is made by adding 4 to each number

63. The correct answer is (A). The pattern in this series is made by adding consecutive odd numbers 3,5,7,9 ... from each number to get the next number, so $63+9 = 72$.

64. The correct answer is (C). Determine the amount of money for (P), (Q), and (R). Then test the alternatives given to see which is correct.

65. The correct answer is (A). (P) is 0.925; (Q) is 0.7142; (R) is 2.223. Clearly (P) is less than (R) but greater than (Q).

66. The correct answer is (B). The cube of 6 is 216. 216 divided by 3 = 72.

67. The correct answer is (D). The sum of $12 + 19 + 7 + 14 + 8 = 60$. The average $60 \div 5 = 12$. $\frac{1}{4}$ of 12 = 3.

68. The correct answer is (B). Determine how much of each part is shaded. Then test each alternative to see which is correct.

69. The correct answer is (B). The pattern in this series is +2, +4, +2, +4, and so on.

70. The correct answer is (D). Determine the amounts for (P), (Q), and (R). Here, (P) = 18, (Q) = 18, and (R) = 42. When you test each alternative to see which is correct, you see that choice (D) is the correct answer: (R) is greater than (P).

71. The correct answer is (A). The pattern in this series is +1, ×2, +1, ×2, and so on.

72. The correct answer is (C). Start by finding 9% of 900: $0.09 \times 900 = 81$. Then subtract 3: $81 - 3 = 78$.

73. The correct answer is (B). The square of 12 is 144. 144 divided by $6 = 24$.

74. The correct answer is (C). Begin with $\frac{1}{4}$ of 32. Then, $8 - 7 = 1$.

75. The correct answer is (B). $4 \times 15 \div 5 = 4 \times 3 = 12$.

76. The correct answer is (C). The pattern in this series is $-9, -7, -5, -3$, and so on.

77. The correct answer is (C). The pattern in this series is made by adding 3 to each number.

78. The correct answer is (C). Begin with $\frac{1}{4}$ of 20. Then, $5 \times 6 = 30$.

79. The correct answer is (C). Let the number be x then x times $4 = 19 - 7$. Therefore, $4x = 12$, $x = 3$.

80. The correct answer is (D). Let the number be x then $x \div 4 = 12 + 8$. Therefore, $x = 20 \times 4$, $x = 80$.

81. The correct answer is (C). Here $2x + 2y + 3x = 5x + 2y$, hence (P) plus (R) is equal to (Q).

82. The correct answer is (D). The pattern in this series is $\times 2, +1, \times 2$, and so on.

83. The correct answer is (D). Let x be the number is subtracted 5. Then, $x - 5 = \frac{1}{3} \times 24$, $x = 13$.

84. The correct answer is (A). Let x be the number then $x \times \frac{1}{3} = 7 \times 2$, therefore, $x = 42$.

85. The correct answer is (D). Let x be the number then $x + 2 = \frac{4}{5} \times 10$, therefore, $x = 6$.

86. The correct answer is (A). The given graph shows us (A) is the correct option.

87. The correct answer is (B). The pattern in this series is square of the number, +1 with the previous number, square of the number, and so on. Hence the next number is 25.

88. The correct answer is (B). Let x be the number, then 4 times of x is $4x$ and 1/4th time of $4x$ is x, hence $x = 20$.

89. The correct answer is (D). Let x be the number, then $x = \frac{5}{9} \times 27 + 20$, therefore $x = 350$.

90. The correct answer is (C). The number is $4^2 + 9 = 25$.

91. The correct answer is (D). The pattern in this series is +6, ×2, +6, ×2, and so on.

92. The correct answer is (C). Let x be the number, then $\frac{1}{4} \times x + 7 = 2 \times 6$, then $x = 20$.

93. The correct answer is (C). Two non-perpendicular and non-parallel lines are called oblique lines.

94. The correct answer is (A). 5% of 250 = 250 × 0.05 = $12\frac{1}{2}$.

95. The correct answer is (C). Triangle has three sides.

96. The correct answer is (B). The cube root if 1728 is 12.

97. The correct answer is (C). Subtraction of two sets = {A, C}.

98. The correct answer is (B). The tenth-place digit of the number 1729.0429 is 0.

99. The correct answer is (B). The decimal value of $\frac{4}{5}$ is 0.80.

100. The correct answer is (C). $\angle BCD = 70°$, $\angle ABC = 20°$, $so \angle C = 180° - 70° = 110°$. Therefore, $\angle A = 180° - 70° - 110° = 50°$

101. The correct answer is (C). The union of two sets = {P, E, N, C, I, L}.

102. The correct answer is (D). The solution is 4 × 16 = 64.

103. The correct answer is (B). The reciprocal of a $\frac{12}{7}$ is $\frac{7}{12}$.

104. The correct answer is (B). The circumference of the circle = πd unit where d is the diameter, therefore circumference = 4π cm.

105. The correct answer is (A). $1 = 100c, then the ratio of 50c and 170c is = 5 : 17.

106. The correct answer is (B). There is no natural number between 0 and 1.

107. The correct answer is (B). 1 week = 7 days, then the ratio of 5 days and 7 days is equal to 5 : 7.

108. The correct answer is (B). 1 yard = 36 inch, then 2 yards = 72 inches. Then the ratio between 72 inch and 18 inch = 72 : 18 = 4 : 1.

109. The correct answer is (C). The correct option is $x^2 + ax = x(x + a)$.

110. The correct answer is (B). $14^2 = 196$ and $15^2 = 225$. Then 205 is between 14 and 15.

111. The correct answer is (C). Since 0.01 is greater than 0.20.

112. The correct answer is (A). The length of MN = 3 cm.

Reading Comprehension Skills

113. The correct answer is (A). See sentence 1.

114. The correct answer is (C). See sentence 2.

115. The correct answer is (B). See sentence 1.

116. The correct answer is (D). The entire passage talks about how evolution happened through natural selection which was the result of tiny changes over the course of time.

117. The correct answer is (B). The first sentence in the passage indicated years 1809–1882 beside Charles Darwin's name.

118. The correct answer is (A). The passage did not state when the theory of evolution was invented.

119. The correct answer is (C). Variety means the quality or state of being different or diverse.

120. The correct answer is (D). Suited means right or appropriate for a particular person, purpose, or situation.

121. The correct answer is (C). The last sentence talked about Charles Darwin's theory.

122. The correct answer is (A). Letter A is the part containing the verb and stating something about the subject.

123. The correct answer is (B). The word <u>dripping</u> is an adjective describing the state of the dagger which means very wet.

124. The correct answer is (A). The word <u>shuddering</u> closely means trembling or quivering with fear, dread, cold, etc.

125. The correct answer is (C). Vanity has different meanings, and all choices are the meanings of the word <u>vanity</u> depending on which is referred. On the poem, the word <u>vanity</u> refers to a heartbreak which can be due to a disappointment by unfulfilled dreams, hopes, or goals.

126. The correct answer is (C). The word <u>lingered</u> is the past tense for the verb linger which means to stay in a place longer than necessary because of a reluctance to leave.

127. The correct answer is (D). The poem was about the symbol of the old man's tattoo. It was about his lost love and has remained hurt by his heartbreak and pride, but toward the end the speaker observed that he was just like the rest of us and that your physical appearance does not define your soul.

128. The correct answer is (B). To reckon is to consider or regard something in a specified way.

129. The correct answer is (A). Ornery means bad-tempered and combative which is synonymous with stubborn.

130. The correct answer is (A). The Blue Heart depicts a classic representation of heart, colored blue. It can be used to express love, support, admiration, happiness, and excitement.

131. The correct answer is (B). See sentence 5.

132. The correct answer is (C). See sentence 6.

133. The correct answer is (D). See sentence 10.

134. The correct answer is (A). According to sentence 3, they can form near the ocean (sea cliffs), high in mountains, or as the walls of canyons and valleys.

135. The correct answer is (D). The matter that settles to the bottom of a liquid, dregs is called sediment.

136. The correct answer is (C). Weathering is the subject of the sentence and is a name of the process described.

137. The correct answer is (A). See sentence 9.

138. The correct answer is (B). To tumble is to (of something abstract) fall rapidly in amount or value.

139. The correct answer is (B). To leap means to jump or spring a long way, to a great height, or with great force.

140. The correct answer is (C). Carousing, as a noun, is the activity of drinking alcohol and enjoying oneself with others in a noisy, lively way.

141. The correct answer is (B). It is fitting that the person who called him out would be having a good time as supported by the description of the speaker about the people's actions which involved leaping and carousing.

142. The correct answer is (A). The poem's title and first line are related to how high the speaker/person thinks of himself over those who he thinks is below him. Later, the poem revealed that he also is of the same level as the people he looked down on.

143. The correct answer is (C). To probe means to seek to uncover information about someone or something.

144. The correct answer is (C). Simile is a figure of speech involving the comparison of one thing with another thing of a different kind, used to make a description more emphatic or vivid. This figure of speech uses the word "like" when comparing.

145. The correct answer is (B). Personification is the attribution of a personal nature or human characteristics to something nonhuman, or the representation of an abstract quality in human form. In this phrase, the speaker is talking about the word <u>poem</u> as if it was a person with a room.

146. The correct answer is (D). Across is one of the prepositions of place.

147. The correct answer is (D). Across means on the other side of something, or from one side to the other of something which has sides or limits such as a city, road, or river. Synonyms include over, beyond, and past.

148. The correct answer is (A). "Introduction to Poetry" suggests that reading poetry doesn't have to be the joylessly analytical exercise so many people think it is. Afterall, interpretations vary from one person to another.

149. The correct answer is (B). The statement is an idiomatic expression used when someone is too busy. If you burn the candle at both ends, you try to do too many things in a short period of time so that you must stay up very late at night and get up very early in the morning to get them done.

150. The correct answer is (B). A foe is an enemy or opponent.

151. The correct answer is (C). The subject of the sentence is the candle. The sentence is referring to how the candle, even though it burns both ends, gives off a lovely light.

152. The correct answer is (A). "First Fig" uses the metaphor of burning a candle at both ends to describe a person living life in the fast lane. The author addresses her enemies and her friends and tells them that she makes a "lovely light".

Vocabulary

153. The correct answer is (D). Empathy is defined as the ability to sense other people's emotions, coupled with the ability to imagine what someone else might be thinking or feeling.

154. The correct answer is (B). The word <u>aesthetic</u> is used as an adjective which is defined as concerned with beauty or the appreciation of beauty.

155. The correct answer is (A). Camaraderie means mutual trust and friendship among people who spend a lot of time together.

156. The correct answer is (B). Impetuous is acting or done quickly and without thought or care.

157. The correct answer is (C). Ostentatious is characterized by vulgar or pretentious display; designed to impress or attract.

158. The correct answer is (A). Being resilient means able to withstand or recover quickly from difficult conditions.

159. The correct answer is (D). Reclusive means avoiding the company of other people; solitary.

160. The correct answer is (D). Parched means extremely thirsty or dried out with heat.

161. The correct answer is (B). Transient means lasting only for a short time; impermanent.

162. The correct answer is (C). Being venerable is being accorded a great deal of respect, especially because of age, wisdom, or character.

163. The correct answer is (A). Wary is feeling or showing caution about possible dangers or problems.

164. The correct answer is (C). Ephemeral is an adjective which means lasting for a very short time. It is also a name for a plant with the same characteristic as described by the adjective.

165. The correct answer is (B). Tyranny means cruel and oppressive government or rule.

166. The correct answer is (C). Vengeance is infliction of injury, harm, humiliation, or the like in return for an injury or other offense received; revenge.

167. The correct answer is (A). Immense is synonymous to vast which means of very great extent or quantity.

168. The correct answer is (B). Liability can mean a legal or regulatory risk or obligation and is synonymous with responsibility.

169. The correct answer is (A). Monotony is lack of variety.

170. The correct answer is (D). Sensible means having, using, or showing good sense or sound judgment.

171. The correct answer is (A). Eschew means to keep away from, shun, or avoid.

172. The correct answer is (C). Preclude means to exclude or debar from something.

173. The correct answer is (B). Deplore means to feel or express deep grief for or in regard to.

174. The correct answer is (A). Tumult is a violent and noisy commotion or disturbance of a crowd or mob; uproar.

Mathematics Concepts

175. The correct answer is (A). The prime factorization of 20 is $= 2 \times 2 \times 5$.

176. The correct answer is (C). The intersection between two sets $= \{W,A,R,E\}$.

177. The correct answer is (A). The associative property $= p.(r.q) = (p.r).q$.

178. The correct answer is (B). The solution is $16 - 4\frac{3}{4} = 11 + (1 - \frac{3}{4}) = 12\frac{1}{4}$.

179. The correct answer is (B). Mr. Smith paid \$624.36 for electric bill for last year, then he paid in one month $= \$\frac{624.36}{12} = \$52.03$.

180. The correct answer is (B). The solution is $7 + (-14) + 6 + (-9) = -10$.

181. The correct answer is (C). Let x be the price of the computer, then 5% of $x = \$80$, then $0.05x = 80$, so $x = 1600$; therefore, the price of the computer with tax is $= \$1,600$. Then the price of the computer without tax $= \$(1600-80) = \$1,520$.

182. The correct answer is (D). The solution is $3\frac{1}{6} + 2\frac{4}{6} = 5\left(\frac{1}{6} + \frac{4}{6}\right) = 5\frac{5}{6}$.

183. The correct answer is (C). The solution for x : $-7 + 8x = 25$, $8x = 32$, therefore $x = 4$.

184. The correct answer is (C). Let x be the principal amount, then S.I. $= \frac{P \times R \times T}{100}$, therefore $P = \frac{100I}{R \times T}$, therefore P = \$800.

185. The correct answer is (A). The proportional ratio: $\frac{Height\ of\ flagpost}{42} = \frac{7}{14}$, then the height of the flag = 21 feet.

186. The correct answer is (C). Here A = 5, B = 3, then $4A + 2B = 4 \times 5 + 2 \times 3 = 26$.

187. The correct answer is (D). The solution $x = 1$.

188. The correct answer is (D). Jones is 14 years old now, 4 years ago his age was 10, 4 years ago his father's age is 4 times of jones age, then his father's age 40 years, now his father's age 40 + 4 = 44 years.

189. The correct answer is (A). The solution $2\frac{4}{3} - 1\frac{2}{3} = 1 + \left(\frac{4}{3} - \frac{2}{3}\right) = 1\frac{2}{3}$.

190. The correct answer is (B). The area of the rectangle = 8 ft. × 12 ft. = 96 ft. The value of the rug is = $4 × 96 = $384.

191. The correct answer is (A). The ratio between $\frac{4}{5}$ and $\frac{9}{10}$ is 8 : 9, that is, 8 to 9.

192. The correct answer is (A). Division, dividend = 3.9276 and divisor = 7.21, therefore the quotient = 0.503 (Approx.)

193. The correct answer is (B). The volume of the solid = 12 × 8 × 4 cc = 384 cc

194. The correct answer is (B). $\frac{2BC}{A} = \frac{2 \times 6 \times 5}{4} = 15$.

195. The correct answer is (D). The solution for x: $4x = 32 \times 5$, then $x = 40$.

196. The correct answer is (D). The multiplication of 62.19 × 0.0763 = 4.742808.

197. The correct answer is (A). The pattern in this series is adding 0.05 after each number and so on. Therefore, the next number is 2.95.

198. The correct answer is (B). The solution for x: $3x = 24$ then $x = 8$.

199. The correct answer is (C). The percentage of 12 over 50 is ($\frac{12}{50} \times 100$)% = 24%.

200. The correct answer is (C). The greatest common factor of 14 and 28 is 14.

201. The correct answer is (D). The multiplication of 72,592 × 190 = 13,792,480.

202. The correct answer is (C). According to the question P − 3 = 5 × 6, hence P = 27.

203. The correct answer is (C). The solution is 18 /12 = $\frac{3}{2}$.

204. The correct answer is (C). ab + 27 = 55, where a = 7, then b = $\frac{28}{7}$ = 4.

205. The correct answer is (C). The area of the triangle = $\frac{1}{2} \times b \times h$ = 144 sq. inch.

206. The correct answer is (C). The solution for x: $x = \dfrac{28}{4} = 7$.

207. The correct answer is (C). The solution for x: $x = \pm 9$.

208. The correct answer is (B). The surface area = $6\,a^2$ sq. unit = $6 \times 6 \times 6$ sq. cm = 216 sq. cm.

209. The correct answer is (B). $\angle ABC = 25°$, $\angle BAC = 90°$, so $\angle BCA = 180° - 115° = 65°$. Therefore, $\angle ACD = 180° - 65° = 115°$.

210. The correct answer is (B). The division of $42 \div \dfrac{1}{6} = 7$.

211. The correct answer is (C). 40% of 100 is 40, and 3 more of 40 is 43.

212. The correct answer is (B). The solution for x: $x > 3$.

213. The correct answer is (C). The solution for x: $x = 9$.

214. The correct answer is (D). The addition of 0.702 + 4.9 + 5.14 = 10.742.

215. The correct answer is (C). The solution x: $x^2 + 25 = 169$, then $x = 12$.

216. The correct answer is (A). The solution for r, where n = 2, r = 42 − 28 = 16.

217. The correct answer is (D). The value of the sides is 8 inches. Then the perimeter is $4 \times 8 = 32$ inches.

218. The correct answer is (A). The square of 15 is 225.

219. The correct answer is (C). The circumference of the circle is = $\pi d = \pi \times 12$ cm = 12π cm.

220. The correct answer is (D). The number increased by 120%, then the number is $80 \times 120\% = 92$.

221. The correct answer is (D). Solving for y, given equations 2x + 3y = 11 and x + y = 3, then solving for y we get y = 5 by multiplying first equation with 2 and subtract both equations we get y = 5.

222. The correct answer is (D). From 7:50 a.m. to 13:40, Jenny was not at her home, then she was not at home for 5 hours and 50 minutes long.

223. The correct answer is (B). The solution for x: $2.5x + 6 = 13.5$. Then $x = 3$.

224. The correct answer is (C). Let x be the number, then $x + 24 = 58$, so $x = 24$.

225. The correct answer is (B). Let x be the number, then 40% of $x = \dfrac{4x}{10}$, therefore, $\dfrac{4x}{10} = 12$, so $x = 30$.

226. The correct answer is (A). The solution for y: $9x - 3y = 3$, at $x = 1$, then $y = 2$.

227. The correct answer is (C). The solution for s: $s = t(8 + 5) - (11 - t)$ at $t = 1$, then $s = 13 - 10 = 3$.

228. The correct answer is (D). 15 times 15 = 225.

229. The correct answer is (C). 15 times 7 = 105, then 105 + 12 = 117.

230. The correct answer is (C). 300% of 90 = 3 times 90 = 270.

231. The correct answer is (A). The correct statement is 5 feet > 4 feet.

232. The correct answer is (C). The pattern in this series is +4, +4, +4, +4, and so on. So, the next number will be 15 + 4 = 19.

233. The correct answer is (C). The multiplication of $6 \times 6 \times 6 \times 6 = 36 \times 36 = 1296$.

234. The correct answer is (D). The solution for y: when $x = 4$ and $y = 7 + 8x$, so, $y = 7 + 24 = 31$.

235. The correct answer is (C). The circumference of the circle is $= \pi d = \pi \times 8$ cm $= 8\pi$ cm.

236. The correct answer is (D). $17^2 = 289$ and $18^2 = 324$. Then 309 is between 17 and 18.

237. The correct answer is (A). Solving for x: $5x - 3x = 11 - 7$, then $x = 2$.

238. The correct answer is (C). The sum of $16 + 13 + 4 + 14 + 8 = 55$. The average $55 \div 5 = 11$.

Language

239. The correct answer is (A). The word <u>fox</u> is a common noun, and therefore, should not be capitalized.

240. The correct answer is (C). The contraction "it's" must be used on the sentence because it is not referring to ownership.

241. The correct answer is (A). The word "their" is a pronoun. The correct word to use is "there".

242. The correct answer is (D). All three statements are grammatically correct. Although each subject sounds plural or seem to be plural, they are all singular. The proper name Karen is also capitalized.

243. The correct answer is (D). Although sentence B seems like question, you may use the exclamation point on any sentence to convey feelings. It is often used in informal language.

244. The correct answer is (A). The correct preposition to use when referring to a surface is "on".

245. The correct answer is (B). The apostrophe for the contraction "can't" is missing.

246. The correct answer is (A). "The United States" is the name of a country, therefore grammatically a singular unit, and would take the singular form. The correct verb to use is "has".

247. The correct answer is (C). Honoring is gerund and is a singular subject. The Ten Commandments is a definite subject which must be capitalized just like book titles. The word "your" is a pronoun and the correct word to use in sentence C is "you're" which is a contraction of "you are".

248. The correct answer is (D). All sentences are grammatically correct and used the appropriate punctuations.

249. The correct answer is (B). "Over" is a preposition used to talk about movement or position at a higher level than something else. Sample: Over the rainbows.

250. The correct answer is (A). Running is a gerund in the sentence. Gerund is a form that is derived from a verb but that functions as a noun.

251. The correct answer is (C). Many is an adjective describing the quantity of the noun "options".

252. The correct answer is (D). By chance also means accidentally which is an adverb.

253. The correct answer is (A). "Her" is a pronoun for a female.

254. The correct answer is (B). "To" is an adverb in the sentence referring to the direction where the bus goes.

255. The correct answer is (C). The word "as" is used as a conjunction in sentence which also means while.

256. The correct answer is (B). The word "quickly" is an adverb which is mostly the form adverbs take. Adverbs describe actions just like how adjectives describe nouns.

257. The correct answer is (B). "For" can be used as a preposition to indicate the object or recipient of a perception, desire, or activity.

258. The correct answer is (A). "About" is used in the sentence to indicate movement in an area.

259. The correct answer is (C). Unable means lacking the skill, means, or opportunity to do something.

260. The correct answer is (B). "This weekend" is an adverb of time which tells us the time when the statement/action will happen.

261. The correct answer is (D). A comma must be placed before the quote and the first word of the quoted sentence must be capitalized.

262. The correct answer is (D). The conjunction that fits the sentence better is neither nor. The noun that is closer to the verb "catches" is singular.

263. The correct answer is (A). The subject "plan" starts with a consonant therefore "an" is not appropriate. It should not be capitalized, too, because the subject is a common noun.

264. The correct answer is (B). The fraction comes before a collective noun and the sentence is describing the action of the subject which are the individual members of the committee. This makes the subject "half of the committee" plural.

265. The correct answer is (A). The fraction comes before a collective noun and the sentence is describing the subject as a group which makes the subject "half of the committee" singular.

266. The correct answer is (C). When using percentages or fraction, the verb will agree to the count of the noun that follows. The word "casts" is plural, and therefore, the correct verb is "are".

267. The correct answer is (C). "Collection" is the subject of the sentence which is singular.

268. The correct answer is (B). Breaking and entering is a compound noun which is singular. The adverb lately indicates that the act has just happened recently.

269. The correct answer is (A). Distances are singular when used as a unit.

270. The correct answer is (B). Sums of money follow a singular verb when used as a unit. However, in this sentence, the sum of the money that have fallen from the bag is plural. Sample: Five dollars is the base fare.

271. The correct answer is (A). For sentences expressing wishes or the contrary, the verb "was" must be replaced by "were" although the count of the subject is singular. Sample: I wish it were summer break. This expresses a subjunctive mood which pairs singular subjects with what we usually think of as plural verbs.

272. The correct answer is (C). Both subjects (Mike and Will; friends) of the compound sentence are plural.

273. The correct answer is (D). The subject is plural which is the "student council members" and the action is in future tense.

274. The correct answer is (B). Kate is a singular subject and the subject of the phrase, "of all the applicants who are applying for the job".

275. The correct answer is (A). The subject of the entire sentence is "Carmen's dogs" which is a plural noun.

276. The correct answer is (D). A comma must come after the phrase "in the end" if a complete sentence follows. "They" is a plural noun and must not be capitalized if is not placed at the beginning of the sentence.

277. The correct answer is (B). The occupation "coach" must not be capitalized unless it is a formal title. For example: President (name of the president of the country). The subject is also singular.

278. The correct answer is (C). When referring to the title of a specific course in university (Heath Aide), you would capitalize it, but you do not capitalize academic subjects (health science program).

Spelling

279. The correct answer is (C). Illiteracy is lack of knowledge in a particular subject: ignorance.

280. The correct answer is (A). Beautiful is the correct spelling.

281. The correct answer is (A). Cooperation is the correct spelling.

282. The correct answer is (N). Nothing is misspelled. Filet is an acceptable spelling. Both filet and fillet mean a strip of boneless meat. Fillet is the more general term, while filet is usually reserved for French cuisine and in the names of French-derived dishes such as filet mignon.

283. The correct answer is (C). Frugivorous is an adjective which is used to describe an animal feeding on fruit.

284. The correct answer is (B). Incessantly means without interruption; constantly.

285. The correct answer is (A). The plural form of innuendo can either be innuendoes or innuendos; similar with tornado.

286. The correct answer is (D). Attention is synonymous with notice, thought, or interest.

287. The correct answer is (C). Bulletin is a short official statement or broadcast summary of news.

288. The correct answer is (A). Evidentiary is another term for evidential which means being, relating to, or affording evidence.

Sentence Composition

289. The correct answer is (B). The action of the statement is present and ongoing.

290. The correct answer is (C). The verb taken is in the past participle form therefore should be preceded by "has been". This action means that this has occurred in the past and is still ongoing.

291. The correct answer is (A). The correct preposition to indicate the length of time of the action is "for".

292. The correct answer is (D). The action of the sentence is in the future.

293. The correct answer is (A). The word "when" is a preposition of time.

294. The correct answer is (C). The word <u>now</u> is an adverb of time. The subject of the first part of the compound sentence is the time, which is singular.

295. The correct answer is (B). The subject of the verb is "speech," which is a singular.

296. The correct answer is (D). The noun nearest to the verb dictates whether it should be plural or singular. Seen is in past participle tense.

297. The correct answer is (C). The noun nearest to the verb dictates whether it should be plural or singular. Seen is in past participle tense.

298. The correct answer is (A). Jump off means to jump down from an elevated point.

HSPT Report

There are 3 types of scores on the HSPT report.

Raw Score

The student receives a point for every correct answer, and there are no penalties for incorrect or omitted answers.

Standard Score

Standard scores are raw scores that have been converted to a standardized scale so they can be statistically analyzed. The conversion process accounts for differences in difficulty levels between multiple forms of the test so that scores are consistent and comparable across forms.

Each subtest and composite score have their own standard score scale. Standard score scales range from 200 to 800, with a mean of 500 and standard deviation of 100.

Standard scores represent equal units of measurement across a continuous scale and are invariant from year to year and edition to edition. Consequently, the standard score scale is an absolute, unchanging frame of reference which permits group comparisons to be made year after year with precision and confidence. If the standard score in a given subject area is higher than the previous year, growth has occurred.

Percentile Rank

To provide additional meaning to a student's standard score, performance is also reported in terms of a percentile rank. In simplest terms, a percentile rank compares a student's performance on the test to some reference group of students within the same grade level. The percentile rank scale ranges from a low of 1 to a high of 99, with 50 being exactly average.

Percentile ranks do not represent actual amounts of achievement, rather, they compare the relative standing of a student with other students. It is important to know that unlike standard scores, percentile ranks are not on an equal interval scale, meaning they do not represent equal units of measure. For example, the difference between percentile ranks 10 and 20 is not the same difference in achievement as the difference between percentile ranks 60 and 70.

The score report will also offer several other performance analyses, including national and local percentiles, standard scores, grade equivalents, and cognitive skills quotients.

High School
Placement Test 2

Verbal Skills

You have 16 minutes to answer the 60 questions in the Verbal Section.

Directions: Choose the best answer for each question.

1. Which among the words below does not belong?

   (A) Weak: week (B) Hour: our (C) Strength: power (D) Poor: pour

2. Which among the words below does not belong?

   (A) Beautiful: scenery (B) Strong: leader (C) Boring: lesson (D) Tiny: small

3. Which among the words below does not belong?

   (A) Who: him (B) How: vigorously (C) When: occasionally (D) Where: downward

4. Which among the words below does not belong?

   (A) Lounge chair (B) Lawn mower (C) Coffee table (D) Magazine

5. Which among the words below does not belong?

   (A) Penny (B) Pound (C) Yen (D) Dollar

6. Kelly can work faster than Luke. Elliot can work faster than Kelly. Luke can work faster than Elliot. If the first two statements are true, then the third is

   (A) True (B) False (C) Unknown

7. Lee wakes up earlier than Jane. Noah wakes up earlier than Jane. Noah wakes up earlier than Lee. If the first two statements are true, then the third is

   (A) True (B) False (C) Unknown

8. Carrie is more stylish than Anna. Sue is more stylish than Carrie. Anna is less stylish than Sue. If the first two statements are true, then the third is

   (A) True (B) False (C) Unknown

9. Bailey's bag is heavier than Luis'. Luis' bag is heavier than Nate's. Nate's bag is heavier than Carmen's. If the second and third sentence are true, then the first sentence is

   (A) True   (B) False   (C) Unknown

10. Rica's ring is more expensive than Natalie's. Natalie's ring is more expensive than Rue's. Rue's ring is more expensive than Tina's. If the first two statements are true, then the third sentence is

    (A) True   (B) False   (C) Unknown

11. Which among the words rhyme with cat?

    (A) Sat   (B) Bet   (C) Dull   (D) Date

12. Which among the words rhyme with feet?

    (A) Fit   (B) Greet   (C) Knit   (D) But

13. Which among the words rhyme with tip?

    (A) Like   (B) Beep   (C) Kit   (D) Bike

14. Which among the words rhyme with reign?

    (A) Hay   (B) Key   (C) Deed   (D) Rain

15. Which among the words rhyme with happily?

    (A) Duty   (B) Beautifully   (C) Pretty   (D) Dainty

16. Which word is synonymous with allude?

    (A) Suggest   (B) Force   (C) Push   (D) Disagree

17. Which word is synonymous with ambiguous?

    (A) Clear   (B) Vague   (C) Precise   (D) Specific

18. Which word is synonymous with candor?

    (A) Guarded   (B) Insincerity   (C) Evading   (D) Truthfulness

19. Which word is synonymous with condone?

    (A) Disregard   (B) Condemn   (C) Punish   (D) None of the above

20. Which word is synonymous with conviction?

    (A) Freedom   (B) Acquittal   (C) Judgment   (D) Innocence

21. Which word is the antonym of confide?

    (A) Impart (B) Leak (C) Divulge (D) Keep

22. Which word is the antonym of deficient?

    (A) Lack (B) Enough (C) Partial (D) Incomplete

23. Which word is the antonym of endow?

    (A) Take (B) Gift (C) Provide (D) Supply

24. Which word is the antonym of entail?

    (A) Include (B) Together (C) Exclude (D) Involve

25. Which word is the antonym of enumerate?

    (A) Subtract (B) Count (C) List (D) Add up

26. Money is to bank as letters is to

    (A) Envelope (B) Post office (C) Park (D) Box

27. Reflect is to contemplate as shadow is

    (A) Darken (B) Illuminate (C) Cerebrate (D) Enlighten

28. Day is to night as sunrise is to

    (A) Morning (B) Early (C) Sun (D) Sunset

29. Lipstick is to lips as eye shadow is to

    (A) Teeth (B) Make-up (C) Eyelids (D) Pallet

30. Computer is to electronics as hammer is to

    (A) Carpentry (B) Tool (C) Metal (D) Wood

31. Which among the words does not belong?

    (A) Roof (B) Ceiling (C) Trough (D) Vent

32. Which among the words does not belong?

    (A) Sail (B) Car (C) Bow (D) Mast

33. Which among the words does not belong?

    (A) Boat   (B) Train   (C) Plane   (D) Chair

34. Which among the words does not belong?

    (A) Plane   (B) Helicopter   (C) Jet ski   (D) Hot air balloon

35. Which among the words does not belong?

    (A) Fish   (B) Snake   (C) Lizard   (D) Crocodile

36. Box is to cube as ice-cream cone is to

    (A) Ice-cream   (B) Wafer   (C) Brown   (D) Cone

37. Water is to liquid as stone is to

    (A) Rock   (B) Small   (C) Solid   (D) Earth

38. Four is to two as thirty-six is to

    (A) Number   (B) Six   (C) Many   (D) Old

39. One is to three as two is to

    (A) Even   (B) Four   (C) Couple   (D) Pair

40. Levitate is to fly as descend is to

    (A) Fall   (B) Lift   (C) Ascend   (D) Climb

41. Valeria <u>furiously</u> told Jim to back-off. The underlined word is a/an

    (A) Adjective   (B) Verb   (C) Adverb   (D) Pronoun

42. <u>When</u> the lights go out, the fireflies flood the rivers. The underlined word is a/an

    (A) Conjunction   (B) Adjective   (C) Verb   (D) Preposition

43. I hear the sound of his heavy breathing as he falls into a <u>deep</u> sleep. The underlined word is a/an

    (A) Noun   (B) Pronoun   (C) Adverb   (D) Adjective

44. My days are filled with <u>happiness</u> now that you're here. The underlined word is a/an

    (A) Adjective   (B) Noun   (C) Adverb   (D) Conjunction

45. The joyful are the ones who succeed in life. The underlined word is a/an

    (A) Adjective (B) Adverb (C) Noun (D) Verb

46. Which best describes the word antebellum?

    (A) Existing before a war (B) The fact or state of being independent (C) The condition of being imprisoned or confined (D) None of the above

47. Which best describes the word auspicious?

    (A) No chance of winning (B) Showing or suggesting that future success is likely (C) Not lucky enough (D) None of the above

48. Which best describes the word churlish?

    (A) Reserved from public embarrassment (B) Shameful (C) Marked by a lack of civility or graciousness (D) None of the above

49. Which best describes the word epiphany?

    (A) None of the choices (B) Not realized by the host (C) Unknown to everyone (D) An illuminating discovery, realization

50. Which best describes the word feckless?

    (A) None of the choices (B) The powerhouse (C) Lack initiative (D) The go-to person

51. Which does not belong to the group?

    (A) Hymn (B) Capital (C) Answer (D) Knowledge

52. Which does not belong to the group?

    (A) Fasten (B) Doubt (C) Debt (D) Plumber

53. Which does not belong to the group?

    (A) Honest (B) Scheme (C) Rhythm (D) None of the above

54. Which does not belong to the group?

    (A) Comb (B) Cat (C) Bet (D) Bat

55. Which does not belong to the group?

    (A) Kick (B) Steer (C) Subtle (D) Tip

56. Which of the words below does not belong with the others?

(A) Think: thought   (B) Dance: danced   (C) Talk: talked   (D) Laugh: laughed

57. Which of the words below does not belong with the others?

(A) Speak: spoke   (B) Ride: rode   (C) Jump: jumped   (D) Come: came

58. Which of the words below does not belong with the others?

(A) Is: are   (B) Has: have   (C) Runs: run   (D) Catch: caught

59. Which of the words below does not belong with the others?

(A) Do: don't   (B) Has: have   (C) Can: can't   (D) Will: won't

60. Which of the words below does not belong with the others?

(A) Calm   (B) Loud   (C) Noisy   (D) Clamorous

End of section.

If you have any time left, go over the questions in this section only.

Do not start the next section.

You have 30 minutes to answer the 52 questions in the Quantitative Skills Section.

Directions:

Choose one answer—the answer you think is best—for each problem.

---

61. What is the average of 6 + 13 + 27 + 2?

    (A) 48   (B) 14   (C) 12   (D) 16

62. Look at the series: 29, 32, 35, _____, 41. What will be the number to fill the blanks?

    (A) 37   (B) 38   (C) 39   (D) 40

63. $5^2 + 12^2 =$

    (A) 13^2 (B) 17^2 (C) 18^2 (D) 14^2

64. Examine the triangle and find the correct option.

    (A) $\angle ACB$ is a right angle   (B) $AC \perp BC$ (C) $\angle BCA$ is a obtuse angle   (D) $\angle B$ is a right angle

65. Examine the images and find the best answer.

    (A) (P) plus (Q) is equal to (R)   (B) (P) is greatest   (C) (R) is smallest   (D) (Q) is less than (P)

66. What number 5 more than the cube of 6 divided by 4?

    (A) 221   (B) 121   (C) 64   (D) 59

67. What number is 4 less than 60% of 20?

(A) 12   (B) 16   (C) 8   (D) 6

68. Look at the series: 2, 9, 18, 25, 34, ____. What number should come next?

(A) 43   (B) 40   (C) 41   (D) 45

69. Let A = {x : x ∈ [0, 2], x is an integer} then the number of elements of A.

(A) 0   (B) 1   (C) 2   (D) 3

70. Examine the best answer.

(P) 6^3 (Q) 3^6 (R) $2^3 \times 6^3$

(A) (P) x (Q) is greater than (R)   (B) (P) – (Q) is an irrational number

(C) (P) is the greatest number   (D) None of these.

71. What number added to 20 is 2 times the product of 9 and 3?

(A) 54   (B) 34   (C) 24   (D) 44

72. What number divided by 8 is $\frac{1}{6}$ of 96?

(A) 64   (B) 128   (C) 192   (D) 160

73. What number is 15 more than $\frac{7}{9}$ of 81?

(A) 63   (B) 78   (C) 74   (D) 68

74. What number added to 4 is 3 times the product of 6 and 2?

(A) 36   (B) 40   (C) 32   (D) 28

75. Look at the series: 4, 5, 9, 10, 14, 15, ____. What number should come next?

(A) 19   (B) 16   (C) 20   (D) 21

76. What number multiplied by 4 is 6 less than 34?

(A) 8   (B) 28   (C) 7   (D) 27

77. Examine (P), (Q), (R) and find the best answer.

(P) 20% of 90   (Q) 90% of 20   (R) 14% of 300

(A) (P) plus (Q) is greater than (R)   (B) (P), (Q), and (R) are equal   (C) (P) is greater than (R)

(D) (R) is greater than (P)

78. What number is 4 times $\frac{1}{4}$ of 40?

    (A) 5 (B) 40 (C) 10 (D) 16

79. Find circumference of the circle whose diameter is 5 cm.

    (A) 10π cm (B) 5π cm (C) 25π cm (D) 50π cm

80. Examine (P), (Q), and (R) and find the best answer

    (P) 2x + 2y + z   (Q) 2(x + z) + y where x, y, z > 0   (R) 2(x + y + z)

    (A) (P) plus (Q) is less than (R)   (B) (R) is the largest number   (C) (P) is the smallest number

    (D) (Q) is greater than (R)

81. Look at the series: 7, 14, 16, 32, 34, ____. What number should come next?

    (A) 36 (B) 72 (C) 68 (D) 64

82. Examine (P), (Q), and (R) and find the best answer.

    (P) 5^4 (Q) 4^5 (R) 3^6

    (A) (P) > (Q) > (R)   (B) (Q) is the largest number   (C) (Q) < (R)   (D) (P) is the largest number

83. What number is 5 times $\frac{1}{2}$ of 60?

    (A) 30 (B) 6 (C) 36 (D) 5

84. If $\frac{2x}{10} = \frac{16}{20}$; then x =

    (A) 16 (B) 8 (C) 4 (D) 2

85. IF A = {0, 1, 2, 3, 4, 5, 6}, then the number of element of A =

    (A) 6 (B) 7 (C) 8 (D) 10

86. If S = t(5 + 6) − (11 − 2t), then find S when t = 1.

    (A) 3 (B) 2 (C) 1 (D) 0

87. Find ∠ABC

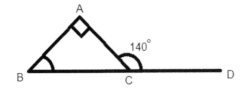

    (A) 40^0 (B) 70^0 (C) 50^0 (D) 90^0

88. 30% of 400 =

    (A) 30 (B) 12 (C) 120 (D) 300

89. Which symbol belongs in the box?

    $0.06 \boxed{} \dfrac{1}{36}$

    (A) < (B) > (C) = (D) ≥

90. What is 0.3742 rounded to nearest hundredth?

    (A) 0.38 (B) 0.3 (C) 0.374 (D) 0.37

91. Which is greatest?

    (A) 4 point (B) 8 quarts (C) 1 gallon (D) 15 cups

92. Which of the following is true?

    (A) 0.007 > 0.07 (B) 2.5 > 2.554 (C) 3.762 > 3.7 (D) 0.9 > 0.87

93. Look at the series: 75, 79, 83, 87, ____. What will be the next number?

    (A) 88 (B) 89 (C) 91 (D) 99

94. The greatest common factor of 36 and 49 is

    (A) 7 (B) 6 (C) 9 (D) 1

95. Examine the circle graph and find the best answer.

    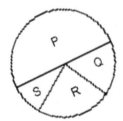

    (A) P is the smallest (B) Q is smaller than S (C) R is largest than S

    (D) P is smallest than R

96. Solve for x: $2x + 5 = 17$

    (A) $x = 12$ (B) $x = 11$ (C) $x = 6$ (D) $x = 5$

97. 30 is 12% of what number?

    (A) 205 (B) 520 (C) 120 (D) 250

98. Examine and find the best answer.

(A) $4^2 > 2^4$ (B) $5^2 > 2^5$ (C) $6^2 > 2^6$ (D) $2^7 > 7^2$

99. 12% of 200 =

(A) 12 (B) 24 (C) 36 (D) 48

100. Look at the series 2, 7, 12, 17, ____. What number should come next?

(A) 18 (B) 22 (C) 20 (D) 19

101. Solve the operation
$2 + (6 \times 4) \div 8$

(A) 3 (B) 5 (C) 7 (D) 9

102. Look at the series: 6, 7, 9, 10, 12, 13, ____. What number should come next?

(A) 14 (B) 1 (C) 16 (D) 18

103. The ratio of $1 and 70¢ is

(A) 1 : 70 (B) 10 : 70 (C) 10 : 7 (D) 1 : 7

104. What number is 6 times $\frac{1}{4}$ of 16?

(A) 42 (B) 24 (C) 36 (D) 16

105. How many natural numbers are between 0 to 4?

(A) 0 (B) 1 (C) 2 (D) 3

106. As a decimal $\frac{9}{10}$ is

(A) 0.75 (B) 0.80 (C) 0.90 (D) 0.95

107. Simplify $(-5)^2 (5)$

(A) –125 (B) 25 (C) –25 (D) 125

108. Solve for y : x + 4y = 21, where x = 1

(A) y = 4 (B) y = 5 (C) y = 20 (D) y = 10

109. What number is cube of 8 divided by 4?

(A) 128 (B) 64 (C) 516 (D) 256

110. What will be 4 less, 10% of 810?

    (A) 84   (B) 81   (C) 78   (D) 77

111. Look at the series 1, 3, 5, 7, ____. What number should come next?

    (A) 17   (B) 13   (C) 11   (D) 9

112. What number divided by 5, leaves 7 more

    (A) 15   (B) 60   (C) 75   (D) 90

End of section.

If you have any time left, go over the questions in this section only.

Do not start the next section.

You have 25 minutes to answer the 62 questions in the Reading Comprehension and Vocabulary Sections.

> ## Directions:
> Read each passage carefully and choose the best answer for each question.

"Hats and Newspapers" by Kathryn Curto

I wear beanies.

When I tug that soft circle of wool onto my head and down over my ears, I'm twenty years younger. In my forties, that may have been the reason for loving them, but not anymore. The fifties are different. Now I just adore the way my head feels held together and pleasantly compressed. Like a girdle for my thoughts. And God knows, they need support.

Then there's this: I'm hopelessly devoted to reading the actual newspaper. And I call it the paper. This makes me even more hopeless and devoted.

But the newspaper and the hat together? That hasn't happened in decades.

My father called me names, made me cry, and one time even threw my plate of Easter frittata at the wall because he said I was being fresh. But he was the best newspaper hat maker ever. When we made them together, mean names and hot tears and broken plates of frittata melted from my view.

What I saw instead: Ink-stained, rolling fingers folding paper creases with care. Hands guiding mine, never pressing hard, never pinching or hurting. Thin smoke lines from his cigarette in the ashtray, rising from its tip.

Unforgettable.

They were newspaper masterpieces. Edges, crisp and sharp. Corners, tight. I remember trying to read the headlines when they were done.

"C'mere closer, doll," he'd say.

Then he'd take a long drag, exhale, place the hat on my head and wink. Those were good days. When my father's corners were loose. Edges soft.

113. Who is the speaker of the short narrative?

(A) The author as a daughter   (B) The father   (C) The mother   (D) The reader

114. Who does the author dedicate the memory to?

(A) Her mother   (B) Her father   (C) Her siblings   (D) Her children

115. What does the phrase "like a girdle for my thoughts" mean?

    (A) Encourage creative thoughts   (B) Promote critical thinking   (C) Contain her thoughts

    (D) Imagine

116. What activity did the author and her father consider the most memorable according to her narrative?

    (A) Her father calling her names   (B) Her father making him cry

    (C) Her father throwing her plate of Easter frittatas   (D) Them making the newspaper hats together

117. What does the author refer to as "the paper"?

    (A) Newspaper   (B) Hat   (C) Beanie   (D) Not long enough

118. What is the narrative all about?

    (A) The author remembering the good old days with her father   (B) How her father made newspaper hats

    (C) How her father called her names, made her cry, and threw her plates of frittatas

    (D) How her father smokes

119. What does the contraction c'mere mean?

    (A) Come over   (B) Come near   (C) Come here   (D) None of the above

120. What is the overall emotion of the narrative?

    (A) Joyous   (B) Expecting   (C) Disappointed   (D) Reminiscence

121. What is the name of the author?

    (A) Father   (B) Kathryn Curto   (C) Mother   (D) Anonymous

122. What verb tense is used in paragraph 4?

    (A) Present   (B) Future   (C) Past   (D) Perfect future

"Lessons Learned" by Diane Malk

When I was young, one of my kindergarten classmates asked me, "Why did you kill Jesus?" I didn't know how to respond. First of all, I wasn't really sure who Jesus was, and secondly, I was pretty sure I hadn't killed anyone. Not lately, anyway.

When I got home that day and told my mother about the incident, she sighed and said it was complicated — she'd explain it to me someday. Meanwhile, I shouldn't worry.

A few months later, it was time for our annual winter pilgrimage to northern California to visit my grandparents. After closing the last suitcase, my mother sat down on the bed and firmly announced, "When we visit Grandma and Grandpa this year, I don't want you spouting off about the little Christmas tree we have. And as long as we're on the subject you need to know that there's no such thing as the Easter Bunny and there's no Santa Claus—remember, we're Jewish!"

This was a lot of information to take in at the time. I had no idea what the statement meant, but it didn't sound good. Besides, I liked having the little tree with all the colorful blinking lights. When my uncle had noticed me looking longingly at our neighbors' Christmas trees, he handed money to my father and said, "Go get that child a tree."

So there it stood, tucked away in a corner of the living room—our first and last Christmas tree.

My mother was justified in forewarning me, since religion was an important aspect of my California grandparents' lives. My grandfather had fled Lithuania as a young boy due to his religion.

My mother continued, "We don't want to upset them with our heathen ways."

"Heathen?" I asked.

"Your grandparents are Orthodox, they go to temple every week. We are Reform. We only go twice a year. We're more like Jews Lite."

"Oh." I nodded and pretended I understood just so I could get back to doing whatever it was I was doing before.

So, I kept my mouth shut during that trip and occupied myself by spinning the dreidel and pondering the fact that we were different. And if anyone asked me again why I killed their Lord, I'd just say he lived way back in history and I never met him.

123. What is the name of the author?

   (A) Orthodox   (B) Diane Malk   (C) Jewish   (D) Mother

124. At what age did the author encounter her first religious confusion?

   (A) Kindergarten   (B) Thirteen years old   (C) Teenage   (D) Late forty's

125. Which word best describes pilgrimage?

   (A) Music concert   (B) Coachella   (C) Journey to a shrine or a sacred place   (D) Debate

126. "When we visit Grandma and Grandpa this year, I don't want you <u>spouting off</u> about the little Christmas tree we have." Which word best describes the underlined word?

   (A) Irresponsibly speak of   (B) Thoughtfully talk about   (C) Keep a secret   (D) Intellectually argue

127. "When my uncle had noticed me looking <u>longingly</u> at our neighbors' Christmas trees." Which word best describes the underlined word?

   (A) Unaffected   (B) Not fazed   (C) Craving   (D) Disliking

128. So there it stood, <u>tucked away</u> in a corner of the living room—our first and last Christmas tree. Which word best describes the underlined word?

   (A) Proudly showing off   (B) Centrally located   (C) Strategically displayed   (D) Hidden

129. My mother was justified in <u>forewarning</u> me. Which word best describes the underlined word?

(A) Untold   (B) Unexpectedly   (C) Surprise   (D) Advance warning

130. "We don't want to upset them with our <u>heathen</u> ways." Which word best describes the underlined word?

(A) Acceptable   (B) Rude   (C) Civilized   (D) Christian

131. What was the lesson the author learned?

(A) It is not good to be different   (B) They are different and there are different beliefs   (C) That the Christmas Tree is not good   (D) That her grandparents were Jewish

"Ripple Effect" by Janis Butler Holm

As a little girl reading fairy tales, I came across the word "replied." Though a bookish child, I somehow read "replied" as "rippled," as in

"Because I said so," the prince rippled.

It seemed to me that a handsome prince would speak in a breezy manner; his language would roll trippingly off the tongue. Even as a child, I understood that royalty can be casual about things the rest of us take seriously.

"I've slain the dragon," the prince rippled.

"I'll wake her with a kiss," the prince rippled.

"You will be my queen," the prince rippled.

"Of course, I have a mistress," the prince rippled.

THE END.

132. Which word is synonymous with ripple?

(A) Trickle   (B) Pour   (C) Stream   (D) Wash away

133. What does the essay mainly talk about?

(A) Sexism and how males are taken as they are no matter what they say or do   (B) The author does not know how to read the word "replied"   (C) How royalties can be casual about things regular people talk about seriously   (D) The little girl liked reading fairy tales

"Flood"
By Erin Murphy

I grew up in the capital of the Confederacy, my skin darkened only by the shadows of Monument Avenue. Once the James River flooded and the two whitest boys from my high school ignored warnings and tooled around in a canoe until the waters took them. For days, their buttoned-down faces were shown on the evening news as helicopters swooped and searched.

They were found clinging to a tree, muddy and cold but unhurt. More than a house with a pool in the suburbs. More than tuition at a brick college with a cupola. More than a guided hunting trip to Alaska where you camp in a luxury yurt. That's how much the rescue cost.

They did not think: moonlit bank where my ancestors were unloaded from ships or branch from which bodies once swung. They did not have to. They did not have to question their worth.

134. "ignored warnings and <u>tooled around</u> in a canoe." What does the underlined word mean?

(A) Used up   (B) Drove around   (C) Hung out   (D) Stood by

135. "their <u>buttoned-down</u> faces were shown on the evening news." What does the underlined word mean?

(A) Well-kept   (B) Tidy   (C) Boring   (D) Hidden

136. What is the message of the essay?

(A) Jealousy for attention   (B) The flood   (C) Racism   (D) The rescue was expensive

Excerpt from "Noises Sound Totally Different on Mars than on Earth. Here's Why"

By Stephen Ornes

July 1, 2022 at 6:30 a.m.

Having a conversation on Mars would be difficult. That's partly because Mars can be really cold, and your teeth may be chattering. But it's also because the Red Planet's thin atmosphere of mostly carbon dioxide doesn't carry sound well. In fact, someone speaking next to you on Mars would sound as quiet as if they were talking 60 meters (200 feet) away.

"It's a pretty drastic difference from Earth," says Baptiste Chide. "You don't want to do it." Better to use microphones and a headset, he says, even at close range. Chide is a planetary scientist at Los Alamos National Laboratory in New Mexico. He and his colleagues shared these new findings about sound on Mars in the May 26 issue of Nature.

Chide's team analyzed some of the first sound recordings ever made on the Red Planet. The recordings had been picked up by a microphone on NASA's Perseverance rover. This space robot has been exploring Mars since February 2021.

137. That's partly because Mars can be really cold, and your teeth may be <u>chattering</u>. What does the underlined word mean?

(A) Click uncontrollably   (B) Closed   (C) Fall off   (D) Melt away

138. "It's a pretty <u>drastic</u> difference from Earth." What does the underlined word mean?

(A) Slight   (B) Little   (C) Severe   (D) Less

139. This space robot has been exploring Mars since February 2021. What is the complete verb of the sentence?

(A) Exploring   (B) Has been exploring   (C) Has been   (D) Has

140. This space robot has been exploring Mars since February 2021. What verb tense is used in the statement?

(A) Past tense   (B) Past perfect progressive   (C) Present perfect progressive   (D) Future perfect progressive

141. What makes noise sound totally different on Mars than on Earth?

(A) Its distance from the sun (B) Its thin atmosphere of mostly carbon dioxide (C) Its size

(D) Its revolution

Easy Basic Pancakes

Ingredients

1 cup all-purpose flour (spooned and leveled)

2 tablespoons sugar

2 teaspoons baking powder

1/2 teaspoon salt

1 cup milk

2 tablespoons unsalted butter, melted, or vegetable oil

1 large egg

1 tablespoon vegetable oil

Assorted toppings, such as butter, maple syrup, confectioners' sugar, honey, jams, preserves, sweetened whipped cream, or chocolate syrup

Directions

Preheat oven to 200 degrees; have a baking sheet or heatproof platter ready to keep cooked pancakes warm in the oven. In a small bowl, whisk together flour, sugar, baking powder, and salt; set aside. In a medium bowl, whisk together milk, butter (or oil), and egg. Add dry ingredients to milk mixture; whisk until just moistened (do not overmix; a few small lumps are fine). Heat a large skillet (nonstick or cast-iron) or griddle over medium. Fold a sheet of paper towel in half and moisten with oil; carefully rub skillet with oiled paper towel. For each pancake, spoon 2 to 3 tablespoons of batter onto skillet, using the back of the spoon to spread batter into a round (you should be able to fit 2 to 3 in a large skillet). Cook until surface of pancakes has some bubbles, and a few have burst, 1 to 2 minutes. Flip carefully with a thin spatula, and cook until browned on the underside, 1 to 2 minutes more. Transfer to a baking sheet or platter; cover loosely with aluminum foil and keep warm in oven. Continue with more oil and remaining batter. (You'll have 12 to 15 pancakes.) Serve warm, with desired toppings.

142. What is the recipe for?

(A) Waffle cones (B) Crepe (C) Bread (D) Pancake

143. What is the first step in the directions?

(A) Whisk together flour, sugar, baking powder, and salt (B) Add dry ingredients to milk mixture (C) Whisk together milk, butter, and egg (D) Preheat oven to 200 degrees

144. What do you think is the reason why your answer to question 143 is the first step?

(A) To save time and get the oven ready once ingredients are prepared (B) No sensible reason

(C) To ensure the wet and dry ingredients are mixed well (D) To avoid a clumpy mixture

Excerpt from "Air Conditioning Will Not Save Us"
By Eric Dean Wilson

It keeps happening. Every summer, unprecedented heat surges through cities across the United States—in Washington, Oregon, and Idaho; in Illinois, Indiana, and Ohio; and in Maryland, Virginia, and New Jersey. Last week, a heat wave melted records in Texas with unrelenting highs well into the 100s for days. And just when residents need it most, the electrical grid fails. Every year, hundreds die from heat-related illness in the U.S., and thousands more end up in emergency rooms from heat stress. Compared to other weather-related disasters, the emergency response to extreme heat from U.S. leaders has been minimal. As a result, many places remain unprepared. How, then, do we make our cities more resilient?

The urban heat crisis is not confined to North America, of course. Extreme heat kills more people than any other climate disaster on the planet, including hurricanes, floods, and wildfires. In the U.K., temperatures are reaching 104°F for the first time in recorded history, and the heat is stoking wildfires across Europe. In India, cities inhabited for centuries are now unlivable with highs of 123°F. And, driven largely by carbon emissions from the developed world, climate change is making it worse. Heat waves are getting hotter, they're happening more often, and they're lasting longer. Currently, 2.2 billion people—that's 30% of the world's population—now experience life-threatening heat during at least 20 days of the year, and scientists predict that heat could threaten as many as 66% of human lives by the end of the century. Unlike more cinematic violence, heat is invisible, even as it's more immediate and widespread. That also makes it more dangerous. Nothing but the massive reduction of fossil fuels will slow this trend.

145. What does the underlined word mean?
Every summer, unprecedented heat surges through cities across the United States.

(A) Common (B) Abnormal (C) Normal (D) Regular

146. What does the underlined word mean?
Last week, a heat wave melted records in Texas with unrelenting highs well into the 100s for days.

(A) Intermittent (B) Spasmodic (C) Continuous (D) Decreasing

147. What does the underlined word mean?
How, then, do we make our cities more resilient?

(A) Rigid (B) Sensitive (C) Adaptable (D) Fragile

148. What does the underlined word mean?
The urban heat crisis is not confined to North America, of course.

(A) City (B) Rural (C) Provincial (D) Countryside

149. What does the underlined word mean?
In the U.K., temperatures are reaching 104°F for the first time in recorded history, and the heat is stoking wildfires across Europe.

(A) Fuel (B) Dampen (C) Extinguish (D) Douse

150. What does the underlined word mean?

In India, cities <u>inhabited</u> for centuries are now unlivable with highs of 123°F.

(A) Empty   (B) Occupied   (C) Wild   (D) Unsettled

151. What makes heat more dangerous than more cinematic violence?

(A) Heat is visible, even as it's more immediate and widespread   (B) Heat is invisible, even as it's less immediate and contained   (C) Heat is invisible, even as it's more immediate and widespread   (D) Heat is invisible, even as it's less immediate and localized

152. How will we slow the trend of people experiencing life-threatening heat according to the article?

(A) Massive addition of fossil fuels will slow this trend   (B) A little reduction of fossil fuels will slow this trend   (C) Massive reduction of air conditioning will slow this trend   (D) Massive reduction of fossil fuels will slow this trend

Vocabulary

Directions:

Choose the word that closely means the same as the underlined word.

153. Because her deep <u>antipathies</u> include crumbs under the table, men who put themselves on a pedestal

(A) A strong feeling of dislike   (B) Sincere affection and kindness   (C) Conscious impulse

(D) None of the above

154. Anxious of the <u>austere</u> judge

(A) Kind- looking   (B) Friendly   (C) Stern and cold   (D) None of the above

155. Showed more than what she should for the <u>clout</u>

(A) Embarrassment   (B) Fame   (C) Shame   (D) None of the above

156. Finally, the <u>culmination</u> of 30-years of exploration

(A) None of the choices   (B) Beginning   (C) Planning stage   (D) Climax

157. For permission in <u>deference</u> of to her parent's wishes

(A) None of the choices   (B) Disrespect   (C) Disregard   (D) Humble submission

158. Up for the challenge without <u>demur</u>

   (A) Go with the flow   (B) Objection   (C) Agreement   (D) None of the choices

159. Unintentionally <u>depleting</u> our life savings

   (A) Rapidly increase   (B) Grow profitable   (C) Lessen markedly in value   (D) None of the above

160. In <u>dire</u> need of assistance

   (A) None of the choices   (B) Mild   (C) Slightly   (D) Desperately

161. Stepsisters never missed the chance to <u>disparage</u> her

   (A) Speak slightingly about   (B) Appreciate   (C) Glorify   (D) None of the above

162. <u>Egregiously</u> copied the author's work

   (A) None of the choices   (B) Sloppy   (C) Respectfully   (D) Blatantly

163. <u>Eloquently</u> speaking as if a royalty

   (A) Inarticulate   (B) Fluently   (C) Stammering   (D) None of the above

164. Blocked by an <u>entrenched</u> resistance to change

   (A) Superficial   (B) Ingrained   (C) Brief   (D) None of the above

165. Unaware of his <u>erratic</u> heartbeat

   (A) Unstable   (B) Consistent   (C) Regular   (D) None of the above

166. <u>Expended</u> deep emotions to someone he barely knows

   (A) Give up   (B) Lose   (C) Use up   (D) None of the above

167. Accused of <u>fomenting</u> religious revolution

   (A) None of the choices   (B) Stopping   (C) Cutting off   (D) Provoke

168. A <u>galvanizing</u> speech pushing everyone to act

   (A) Discouraging   (B) Urge   (C) Demotivate   (D) None of the above

169. Facing away from <u>ignominious</u> defeat

   (A) None of the choices   (B) Glorious   (C) Honorable   (D) Humiliating

170. Knew the lovable prince <u>incited</u> the rebellion in the kingdom

    (A) Encouraged   (B) Disallow   (C) Stop   (D) None of the above

171. <u>Abjure</u> his loyalty to the kingdom as a knight and elope with the witch

    (A) Renounce   (B) Solemnly swear   (C) Promise   (D) None of the above

172. Incarcerate the <u>bellicose</u> supporters

    (A) Aggressive   (B) Passive   (C) Silent   (D) None of the above

173. Aware of the <u>deleterious</u> effects of smoking

    (A) Beneficial   (B) Harmless   (C) Harmful   (D) None of the above

174. Ignored the <u>fatuous</u> comment

    (A) Sensible   (B) Silly   (C) Useful   (D) None of the above

End of section.

If you have any time left, go over the questions in this section only.

Do not start the next section.

You have 45 minutes to answer the 64 questions in the Mathematics Concepts Section.

Directions:

Choose one answer—the answer you think is best—for each problem. You may use scratch paper when working on these problems

175. Find the ratio between 7 months and 1 year.

    (A) 7 : 1   (B) 7 : 10   (C) 7 : 12   (D) 12 : 7

176. The square root of 286 is between

    (A) 16 to 17   (B) 17 to 18   (C) 13 to 14   (D) 15 to 16

177. Which one of the following is true?

    (A) 20 < 2.0   (B) −7 > −3   (C) 4 > 0.4   (D) 27 > 41

178. The prime factorization of 48 is

    (A) 2 . 2 . 2 . 2 . 3   (B) 6 . 8   (C) 12 . 4   (D) 4 . 4 . 3

179. Which one of the property is commutative property?

    (A) a . b = a . b   (B) a . b = a + b   (C) a + b = a . b   (D) a . b = b . a

180. {1, 4, 5, 7, 9} ∩ {1, 3, 9, 12} is equal to

    (A) ∅   (B) {1, 9}   (C) {4, 5, 7}   (D) {1, 3, 4, 5, 7, 9, 12}

181. Solve: $12 - 3\frac{2}{3}$

    (A) $9\frac{1}{3}$ (B) $9\frac{2}{3}$ (C) $8\frac{1}{3}$ (D) $8\frac{2}{3}$

182. Mr. Wilson paid $720 for his insurance policy last years. How much money he paid in one month?

    (A) $12   (B) $60   (C) $40   (D) $50

183. Solve: 4 + (−20) + 6 + (−2) =

(A) 22   (B) −22   (C) −10   (D) 10

184. If the 10% sales tax on a Xerox machine was $180, then what is the price of the machine without the tax?

(A) $1,800   (B) $1,620   (C) $1,520   (D) $1,720

185. Solve: $3\dfrac{7}{9} + 3\dfrac{2}{9}$

(A) $11\dfrac{9}{9}$ (B) 11   (C) 10   (D) 19

186. Solve for x : $27 - 4x = 3$, $x =$

(A) 24   (B) 30   (C) 6   (D) 5

187. Ms. Myesha paid $70 as interest on a loan that had 5% interest rate. How much money did she borrow?

(A) $1,200   (B) $1,300   (C) $1,350   (D) $1,400

188. If A = 7, B = 5, then 3A + 4B =

(A) 20   (B) 21   (C) 1   (D) 41

189. $5(7x - 8) = 30$, x =

(A) 1   (B) 2   (C) 3   (D) 4

190. Solve: $2\dfrac{2}{3} - 1\dfrac{4}{3}$

(A) $1\dfrac{1}{3}$ (B) $\dfrac{1}{3}$ (C) $\dfrac{2}{3}$ (D) $1\dfrac{2}{3}$

191. Find the area of the rectangle whose dimension
a = 5 cm, b = 4 cm.

(A) 25 cm²   (B) 16 cm²   (C) 8 cm²   (D) 20 cm²

192. Find the ratio of $\dfrac{10}{13}$ of $\dfrac{5}{4}$.

(A) 13 : 8   (B) 13 : 10   (C) 8 : 13   (D) 10 : 13

193. Solve: $\dfrac{4.278}{8.46}$

(A) 0.5056   (B) 0.5055   (C) 0.5054   (D) 0.5053

194. If A = 4, B = 6, C = 5, then find $\dfrac{5B}{4C}$.

(A) $\dfrac{3}{2}$ (B) $\dfrac{5}{2}$ (C) $\dfrac{5}{3}$ (D) $\dfrac{3}{5}$

195. If $\dfrac{6x}{5} = 48$, then $x =$

(A) 8   (B) 5   (C) 6   (D) 40

196. What is the volume of the solid where height = 10 cm, length = 6 cm, breath = 4 cm

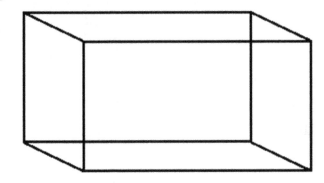

(A) 240 cc   (B) 420 cc   (C) 402 cc   (D) 204 cc

197. Solve 64 × 927

(A) 53,928   (B) 59,328   (C) 52,928   (D) 58,932

198. If A% of 20 is 4, A =

(A) 10%   (B) 40%   (C) 80%   (D) 20%

199. Solve : 5x − 7 = 9x − 43,

(A) x = 9   (B) x = 10   (C) x = 8   (D) x = 11

200. The greatest common factor of 48, 56 is

(A) 6   (B) 7   (C) 8   (D) 12

201. The difference between product of 5 and 3 and the sum of 5 and 3 is

(A) 15   (B) 8   (C) 7   (D) 22

202. Solve : 4 × 2 ÷ (12 ÷ 3)

(A) 8   (B) 12   (C) 6   (D) 2

203. If ab + 56 = 92 and a = 6, then b =

(A) 36   (B) 6   (C) 5   (D) 25

204. Find the area of the square where side is 5 cm.

(A) 5 cm²   (B) 20 cm²   (C) 25 cm²   (D) 10 cm²

205. $\dfrac{7x}{8} + 4 = 32$, then $x =$

(A) 4   (B) 8   (C) 16   (D) 32

206. $x^2 + 9 = 73$, solve for x.

(A) $x = \pm 9$ (B) $x = \pm 8$ (C) $x = \pm 7$ (D) $x = \pm 11$

207. Find the surface area of the cube when base a = 7 cm.

(A) 343 cm²   (B) 294 cm²   (C) 256 cm²   (D) 216 cm²

208. Find $\angle x$

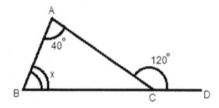

(A) 60⁰   (B) 80⁰   (C) 100⁰   (D) 40⁰

209. Solve $56 \div \dfrac{1}{7} =$

(A) 7   (B) 9   (C) 8   (D) 10

210. What is 5 more than 50% of 80?

(A) 40   (B) 45   (C) 35   (D) 50

211. Solve x : 4x + 3 > 3x + 4

(A) x > 4   (B) x < 4   (C) x > 1   (D) x < 1

212. Solve $5x + 13 = 58$, $x =$

(A) 45   (B) 9   (C) 50   (D) 10

213. Solve $0.902 + 5.9 + 5.26 =$

(A) 16.202   (B) 10.626   (C) 12.062   (D) 10.266

214. $\sqrt{x^2 + 9} = 5, x =$

(A) 16   (B) 4   (C) 25   (D) 5

215. $(8 + 9)^2 =$

(A) 324   (B) 289   (C) 225   (D) 256

216. Find the perimeter of a square whose side is 4 cm

(A) 4 cm   (B) 8 cm   (C) 16 cm   (D) 32 cm

217. $r = 36 - (3 + 4)(x)$, where $x = 1$, $r =$

(A) 36   (B) 7   (C) 43   (D) 29

218. Find the radius whose diameter is 4 cm.

(A) 4 cm   (B) 2 cm   (C) 16 cm   (D) 8 cm

219. $2x + 4y = 10$, $x + y = 2$, then $y =$

(A) 3   (B) −3   (C) 0   (D) 2

220. Increased by 140%, the number 40 becomes

(A) 16   (B) 56   (C) 36   (D) 46

221. What is the cube root of 5832?

(A) 8   (B) 12   (C) 16   (D) 18

222. Elena left her home for school at 8:40 a.m., and she came back after school at 2:40 p.m. How long was she not in her home?

(A) 4 Hrs   (B) 6 Hrs   (C) 5 Hrs   (D) 5 Hrs

223. Solve for x in the following equation:
$4.5x + 6.5 = 15.5$

(A) 2   (B) 3   (C) 4   (D) 6

224. 38 more than a certain number is 64. What is the number?

(A) 72   (B) 26   (C) 24   (D) 23

225. 50% of what number is equal to 16?

(A) 42   (B) 32   (C) 22   (D) 52

226. If $6x - 2y = 4$, and $x = 2$, what does y equal?

(A) 2   (B) 3   (C) 4   (D) 1

227. $s = t(10 + 5) - (10 - t)$ and $t = 2$, what does *s* equal?

(A) 22   (B) 32   (C) 42   (D) 12

228. $25^2 =$

(A) 225   (B) 625   (C) 325   (D) 425

229. $(18 \times 5) + 12 =$

(A) 105   (B) 101   (C) 102   (D) 128

230. 400% of 80 =

(A) 90   (B) 180   (C) 220   (D) 320

231. Which of the following number sentence is true?

(A) 5 feet < 4 feet   (B) 7 feet > 4 feet   (C) 2 feet > 6 feet   (D) 4 feet < 2 feet

232. Look at this series: 4, 7, 10, 13 ... . What number should come next?

(A) 16   (B) 17   (C) 18   (D) 20

233. $(12 - 3)^3 =$

(A) 729   (B) 81   (C) 6561   (D) 512

234. What is the value of y when $x = 3$ and $y = 7 + 8x$?

(A) 24   (B) 37   (C) 31   (D) 41

235. Find the circumference of the circle whose diameter 10 cm

(A) 4π cm   (B) 10π cm   (C) 8π cm   (D) 16π cm

236. The square root of 419 is between

(A) 19 to 20   (B) 20 to 22   (C) 90 to 100   (D) 17 to 18

237. Solve x : 7x + 7 > 5x + 11

(A) x > 2   (B) x > 3   (C) x < 2   (D) x = 2

238. What number is the average of 18, 13, 7, 24, and 8?

(A) 55   (B) 15   (C) 14   (D) 45

End of section.

If you have any time left, go over the questions in this section only.

Do not start the next section.

Language

You have 25 minutes to answer the 60 questions in the Language Section.

Directions:

Look for errors in capitalization, punctuation, or usage. Choose the answer with the errors. If no errors found, choose D.

---

239. (A) The New York is the largest city in the United States.
(B) New York City is the largest city in the United States.
(C) A New York City is the largest city in the United States.
(D) None of the above

240. (A) Adam was the first man on the Earth.
(B) An Adam was the first man on the Earth.
(C) The Adam was a first man on the Earth.
(D) None of the above

241. (A) They're eyes met, and it was love.
(B) There eyes met, and it was love.
(C) Their eyes met, and it was love.
(D) None of the above

242. (A) None of the choices
(B) Their is a saying that goes, "Don't do unto others what you don't want done unto you."
(C) They're is a saying that goes, "Don't do unto others what you don't want done unto you."
(D) There is a saying that goes, "Don't do unto others what you don't want done unto you."

243. (A) They're getting married next month.
(B) Their getting married next month.
(C) There getting married next month.
(D) None of the above

244. (A) Youre' eyes glistened as he spoke words of love.
(B) You're eyes glistened as he spoke words of love.
(C) Your eyes glistened as he spoke words of love.
(D) None of above

245. (A) Honestly, your not someone worth remembering.
     (B) Honestly, you're not someone worth remembering.
     (C) Honestly, youre' not someone worth remembering.
     (D) None of the above

246. (A) None of the choices
     (B) Whethere you like it or not, I will be there.
     (C) Weather you like it or not, I will be there.
     (D) Whether you like it or not, I will be there.

247. (A) The weather forecast said that we'll be expecting a sunny day.
     (B) The whether forecast said that we'll be expecting a sunny day.
     (C) The weathere forecast said that we'll be expecting a sunny day.
     (D) None of the above

248. (A) She talked really fast because she was nervous.
     (B) She talked real fast because she was nervous.
     (C) She talked realy fast because she was nervous.
     (D) None of the above

249. (A) He stood up quicker as if he'd seen a ghost.
     (B) He stood up quick as if he'd seen a ghost.
     (C) He stood up quickly as if he'd seen a ghost.
     (D) None of the above

250. (A) Have you heard of the news?
     (B) Did you heard of the news?
     (C) Has you heard of the news?
     (D) None of the above

251. (A) None of the choices
     (B) She had been sitting on that bench since this morning.
     (C) She have been sitting on that bench since this morning.
     (D) She has been sitting on that bench since this morning.

252. (A) None of the choices
     (B) She had been sitting on that bench since this morning until the rain poured.
     (C) She have been sitting on that bench since this morning until the rain poured.
     (D) She has been sitting on that bench since this morning until the rain poured.

253. (A) I will have been working for 40 years.
     (B) I will has been working for 40 years by the time I retire.
     (C) I will have been working for 40 years by the time I retire.
     (D) None of the above

254. (A) She kept talking about the hole on the wall.
     (B) He placed the papers about the table.
     (C) There is something standing about the window.
     (D) None of the above

255. (A) The dessert is cooler at night.
     (B) The train arrives at any time.
     (C) I was at store when I got your message.
     (D) None of the above

256. (A) None of the choices
     (B) The cake is baking on the oven.
     (C) The cake is baking at the oven.
     (D) The cake is baking in the oven.

257. (A) The freshly baked sweets are over the countertop.
     (B) The freshly baked sweets are on the countertop.
     (C) The freshly baked sweets are in the countertop.
     (D) None of the above

258. (A) The passengers sat with the bus.
     (B) The debris was removed with a tweezer.
     (C) Cookies are placed with biodegradable boxes.
     (D) None of the above

259. (A) Susan had an argument with Paul. She caught Paul texting another girl.
     (B) Susan had an argument with Paul. He caught Paul texting another girl.
     (C) Susan had an argument with Paul. Her caught Paul texting another girl.
     (D) None of the above

260. It's my cousin's <u>birthday</u>.

(A) Adverb   (B) Preposition   (C) Noun   (D) Adjective

261. You get gifts <u>on birthdays</u>.

(A) Adverb   (B) Verb   (C) Noun   (D) Preposition

262. I get tired of <u>running</u> so I just walk.

(A) Verb   (B) Noun   (C) Adjective   (D) Adverb

263. He's seen <u>running</u> for his life.

(A) Noun   (B) Verb   (C) Adjective   (D) Adverb

264. <u>Happy</u> thoughts keep me going.

(A) Noun   (B) Pronoun   (C) Adjective   (D) Verb

265. I will be <u>happily</u> thinking of us while you're away.

(A) Noun   (B) Adverb   (C) Adjective   (D) Preposition

266. <u>Sixty-eight</u> balloons flew to the sky.

(A) Noun   (B) Adjective   (C) Conjunction   (D) Preposition

267. <u>One-fourth</u> is a fraction.

(A) Noun   (B) Adjective   (C) Verb   (D) Pronoun

268. Can you spare a <u>one-fourth</u> sheet of paper?

(A) Noun   (B) Adjective   (C) Verb   (D) Pronoun

269. <u>Violets</u> are one of the cheeriest little flowers to grace the landscape.

(A) Noun   (B) Pronoun   (C) Adjective   (D) Verb

270. He was captivated by her <u>violet</u> eyes.

(A) Noun   (B) Pronoun   (C) Adjective   (D) Verb

271. She runs away as tears <u>stream</u> down her face.

    (A) Noun (B) Pronoun (C) Adjective (D) Verb

272. They walked while holding hands by the <u>stream</u>.

    (A) Noun (B) Pronoun (C) Adjective (D) Verb

273. He took up the courage to <u>face</u> finally his fears.

    (A) Noun (B) Pronoun (C) Verb (D) Adjective

274. His <u>face</u> stunned by the unpleasant surprise.

    (A) Verb (B) Noun (C) Pronoun (D) Adjective

275. Where there <u>is</u> darkness, there is light.

    (A) Verb (B) Noun (C) Pronoun (D) Adjective

276. <u>Are</u> they there yet?

    (A) Noun (B) Pronoun (C) Verb (D) Adjective

277. Are they <u>there</u> yet?

    (A) Noun (B) Pronoun (C) Adverb (D) Adjective

278. Are they there <u>yet</u>?

    (A) Noun (B) Pronoun (C) Adverb (D) Conjunction

Spelling

Directions:

Identify which among the words is spelled incorrectly. If nothing is misspelled, write N on your answer sheet.

279. (A) Knitting
    (B) Wriggle
    (C) Writting
    (D) Billing

280. (A) Sutle
    (B) Doubt
    (C) Debt
    (D) Plumber

281. (A) Aquit
     (B) Acquire
     (C) Lacquer
     (D) Racquet

282. (A) Lacquey
     (B) Picquet
     (C) Sacques
     (D) Acquest

283. (A) Telepresence
     (B) Absense
     (C) Presence
     (D) Essence

284. (A) Huddle
     (B) Headdress
     (C) Cheddar
     (D) Adress

285. (A) Arguement
     (B) Consequence
     (C) Congruence
     (D) Unique

286. (A) Achieve
     (B) View
     (C) Beleive
     (D) Tier

287. (A) Referring
     (B) Robbing
     (C) Orderring
     (D) Stopping

288. (A) Halloween
     (B) Sleep
     (C) Chitah
     (D) Bullet

Sentence Composition

> # Directions:
> Choose the best words to complete the sentences.

289. The _____ of the new king will lead the kingdom back to its glorious days.

    (A) Rein (B) Reign (C) Rain (D) Pain

290. _____, the restock comes later in the afternoon.

    (A) Supposedly (B) Supposably (C) Purportedly (D) Proposedly

291. In case of normal wear and tear, our products are _____.

    (A) Ensured (B) Insured (C) Assured (D) Reassured

292. Their family's _____ reputation surpasses any defamation no matter how small or big.

    (A) Deep-seeded (B) Deep-seated (C) Deep-fitted (D) Deep-sited

293. There is no doubt she'll give him her _____ when they get home after getting caught cheating.

    (A) Piece of (her) mind (B) Peace of mind (C) Peace of heart (D) Peace of body

294. Just before the announcement of winners, the host gave her friends a _____ of the winners.

    (A) Sneak peek (B) Sneak peak (C) Sneek peek (D) Sneek peak

295. She didn't notice that the man asking for directions grabbed her wallet by _____ of hand.

    (A) Slight (B) Sleight (C) Slate (D) Plate

296. The _____ amount of the loan was beyond what they can afford in a lifetime.

    (A) Principle (B) Principal (C) Teacher (D) Student

297. The teacher is _____ to the idea of out-of-country fieldtrip due to recent outbreak.

    (A) Adverse (B) Averse (C) Reverse (D) Converse

298. The media aims to _____ the community of the latest developments of the project.

(A) Apprise   (B) Appraise   (C) Appreciate   (D) Approach

End of section.

If you have any time left, go over the questions in this section only.

ANSWER KEY

1. C	31. B	61. C	91. B	121. B	151. C	181. C	211. C	241. C	271. D
2. D	32. B	62. B	92. D	122. C	152. D	182. B	212. B	242. D	272. A
3. A	33. D	63. A	93. C	123. B	153. A	183. B	213. C	243. A	273. C
4. B	34. C	64. D	94. D	124. A	154. C	184. C	214. B	244. C	274. B
5. A	35. A	65. A	95. C	125. C	155. B	185. B	215. B	245. B	275. A
6. B	36. D	66. D	96. C	126. A	156. D	186. C	216. C	246. D	276. C
7. C	37. C	67. C	97. D	127. C	157. D	187. D	217. D	247. A	277. C
8. A	38. B	68. C	98. D	128. D	158. B	188. D	218. B	248. B	278. D
9. C	39. B	69. D	99. B	129. D	159. C	189. B	219. A	249. C	279. C
10. C	40. A	70. A	100. B	130. B	160. D	190. B	220. B	250. A	280. A
11. A	41. C	71. B	101. B	131. B	161. A	191. D	221. D	251. D	281. A
12. B	42. A	72. B	102. A	132. A	162. D	192. C	222. B	252. B	282. N
13. C	43. D	73. B	103. C	133. A	163. B	193. A	223. A	253. C	283. B
14. D	44. B	74. C	104. B	134. B	164. B	194. A	224. B	254. A	284. D
15. B	45. C	75. A	105. D	135. C	165. A	195. D	225. B	255. A	285. A
16. A	46. A	76. C	106. C	136. D	166. C	196. A	226. C	256. D	286. B
17. B	47. B	77. D	107. D	137. A	167. D	197. B	227. A	257. B	287. C
18. D	48. C	78. B	108. B	138. C	168. B	198. B	228. B	258. B	288. C
19. A	49. D	79. B	109. A	139. B	169. D	199. A	229. C	259. A	289. B
20. C	50. C	80. B	110. D	140. C	170. A	200. C	230. D	260. C	290. A
21. D	51. B	81. C	111. D	141. B	171. A	201. C	231. B	261. A	291. B
22. B	52. A	82. B	112. C	142. A	172. A	202. D	232. A	262. B	292. B
23. A	53. D	83. B	113. A	143. D	173. C	203. B	233. A	263. B	293. A
24. C	54. A	84. C	114. B	144. A	174. B	204. C	234. C	264. C	294. A
25. A	55. C	85. B	115. C	145. B	175. C	205. D	235. B	265. B	295. B
26. B	56. A	86. B	116. D	146. C	176. A	206. B	236. B	266. B	296. B
27. D	57. C	87. C	117. A	147. C	177. C	207. B	237. A	267. A	297. B
28. D	58. D	88. C	118. A	148. A	178. A	208. B	238. C	268. B	298. A
29. C	59. B	89. B	119. C	149. A	179. D	209. C	239. B	269. A	
30. A	60. A	90. D	120. D	150. B	180. B	210. B	240. A	270. C	

NOTE: To calculate Raw score, allocate 1 point for each correct answer and 0 points for each incorrect and unanswered questions.

Number of correct answers = _____ (A)

Number of incorrect or unanswered answers = _____ (B)

Final Raw score = A – B = _____ - _____ = _____

EXPLANATIONS

Verbal Skills

1. The correct answer is (C). A, B, and D are word pairs which sound alike and are called homonyms. Strength and power are synonyms.

2. The correct answer is (D). A, B, and C are word pairs of adjective and nouns they may be used with. Tiny and small are synonyms.

3. The correct answer is (A). B, C, and D are adverbs and the corresponding question the adverbs can answer. A is a question and pronoun pair.

4. The correct answer is (B). A, C, and D are items you see in a living room. A lawn mower is used outdoors.

5. The correct answer is (A). B, C, and D are currencies. A is the United States one-cent coin.

6. The correct answer is (B). Luke works slower than Kelly, so Elliot is the fastest among the three.

7. The correct answer is (C). Both Lee and Noah wake up earlier than Jane, but it is unknown who wakes up earlier between Lee and Noah.

8. The correct answer is (A). Since Sue is the most stylish among the three, it is only true that Anna is less stylish than Sue.

9. The correct answer is (C). There is no proof in the statements whether Bailey's bag is heavier or lighter than Luis'. There is no point of comparison between Bailey and Luis' bags.

10. The correct answer is (C). There is no proof in the statements whether Rue's ring is more expensive than Tina's. There is no point of comparison between Rue and Tina's rings.

11. The correct answer is (A). Cat rhymes with sat. Both words are pronounced with a short *a* sound.

12. The correct answer is (B). Feet rhymes with greet. Both words are pronounced with a long *e* sound.

13. The correct answer is (C). Tip best rhymes with tip. Both words are pronounced with a short *i* sound.

14. The correct answer is (D). Reign and rain are homophones. Rain best rhymes with reign and both are pronounced with a long *a* sound.

15. The correct answer is (B). Beautifully best rhymes with happily as both words end with "-ly".

16. The correct answer is (A). Allude is to suggest or call attention to indirectly, hint at.

17. The correct answer is (B). Ambiguous is open to more than one interpretation: not having one obvious meaning.

18. The correct answer is (D). Candor is the quality of being open and honest in expression: frankness.

19. The correct answer is (A). To condone is to accept and allow (behavior that is considered morally wrong or offensive) to continue.

20. The correct answer is (C). Conviction is a formal declaration that someone is guilty of a criminal offense, made by the verdict of a jury or the decision of a judge in a court of law.

21. The correct answer is (D). To confide is to tell someone about a secret or private matter while trusting them not to repeat it to others.

22. The correct answer is (B). Deficient means lacking in some necessary quality or element.

23. The correct answer is (A). To endow is to furnish freely or naturally with some power, quality, or attribute. If you endow someone something, you give.

24. The correct answer is (C). Entail means to impose, involve, or imply as a necessary accompaniment or result.

25. The correct answer is (A). To enumerate is to ascertain the number of count or to specify one after another: list.

26. The correct answer is (B). This is a sample of object–purpose relationship. The bank is an establishment where money is kept, and the post office is an establishment where letters are sent.

27. The correct answer is (D). This is a sample of a synonym relationship. When you reflect on something, you contemplate; when something is shadowed, it is darkened or shaded.

28. The correct answer is (D). The word combinations are opposites. The opposite of day is night and of sunrise is sunset.

29. The correct answer is (C). This is a sample of object–purpose relationship. Lipstick is used for the lips and eye shadow is used for eyelids.

30. The correct answer is (A). This is a sample of specific–generic relationship. Computer belongs to the category of electronics and hammer belongs to carpentry.

31. The correct answer is (B). A, C, and D are external parts of a house. A ceiling is an internal part of a house.

32. The correct answer is (B). A, C, and D are parts of a boat.

33. The correct answer is (D). A, B, and C are modes of transportation.

34. The correct answer is (C). A, B, and D are aerial modes of transportation. A jet ski is used on bodies of water.

35. The correct answer is (A). B, C, and D are reptiles.

36. The correct answer is (D). A box is a sample of an object in the shape of a cube. An ice-cream cone as described by its name is an object with the shape of a cone.

37. The correct answer is (C). Water is a liquid as a stone is a solid.

38. The correct answer is (B). Two is the square root of four as six is the square root of thirty-six.

39. The correct answer is (B). One and three are consecutive odd numbers, while two and four are consecutive even numbers.

40. The correct answer is (A). Levitate is a synonym of to fly. Descend is a synonym of to fall.

41. The correct answer is (C). Furiously is an adverb describing the manner Valeria told Jim to back off.

42. The correct answer is (A). "When" is used as a conjunction to join two phrases together by suggesting the time the fireflies flood the rivers.

43. The correct answer is (D). Deep is used to describe the quality of sleep. Sleep in the statement is a noun.

44. The correct answer is (B). Happiness is a noun which is a state of well-being and contentment: joy.

45. The correct answer is (C). Joyful in the sentence is the subject and used as a noun. The word is also preceded by the determiner "the".

46. The correct answer is (A). Antebellum means existing before a war especially existing before the American Civil War; antebellum houses; the antebellum South.

47. The correct answer is (B). Auspicious means showing or suggesting that future success is likely; attended by good auspices: fortunate, prosperous.

48. The correct answer is (C). To be churlish means to resemble or characteristic of a churl: vulgar; of, resembling, or characteristic of a churl: vulgar.

49. The correct answer is (D). To have an epiphany is to have an illuminating discovery, realization, a revealing scene, or moment.

50. The correct answer is (C). When someone is feckless, he is someone lacking initiative or strength of character; irresponsible.

51. The correct answer is (B). A, C, and D are words pronounced with a silent letter.

52. The correct answer is (A). B, C, and D are words pronounced with a silent B.

53. The correct answer is (D). A, B, and C are words pronounced with a silent H.

54. The correct answer is (A). A is pronounced with a silent letter, B.

55. The correct answer is (C). C is pronounced with a silent letter, B.

56. The correct answer is (A). B, C, and D are word pairs of verbs where their past tense is formed by adding the suffix -ed.

57. The correct answer is (C). C is the only word pair where its past tense is formed by adding the suffix -ed.

58. The correct answer is (D). A, B, and C are word pairs of present tense singular verb and their plural form.

59. The correct answer is (B). A, C, and D are word pairs of their contractions.

60. The correct answer is (A). B, C, and D are synonyms.

Quantitative Skills

61. The correct answer is (C). The sum of the numbers = 6 + 13 + 27 + 2 = 48. Then the average = $\frac{48}{4} = 12$.

62. The correct answer is (B). The pattern in this series is made by adding 3 to each number.

63. The correct answer is (A). $5^2 + 12^2 = 25 + 144 = 169 = 13^2$.

64. The correct answer is (D). $\angle B$ is an right angle.

65. The correct answer is (A). From the images we can say (P) + (Q) = (R).

66. The correct answer is (D). Cube of 6 = 216. Dividing 216 by 4 is equal to 54, adding 5 more we will get 54 + 5 = 59.

67. The correct answer is (C). 60% of 20 = 0.6 × 20 = 12, 4 less than 12 is equal to = 12 − 4 = 8.

68. The correct answer is (C). The pattern in this series is made by adding +7, +9, +7, +9, and so on.

69. The correct answer is (D). The number of integers between [0, 2] are 0, 1, and 2. Therefore, 3 integers.

70. The correct answer is (A). Obviously (P) × (Q) is greater than (R).

71. The correct answer is (B). The product of 9 and 3 is 27, and 27 times 2 is 54, then the difference between 54 and 20 = 54 − 20 = 34.

72. The correct answer is (B). 96 divided by 6 is = 16, and 16 times 8 = 128.

73. The correct answer is (B). $81 \times \dfrac{7}{9} = 63$. Now adding 63 + 15 = 78.

74. The correct answer is (C). The product of 6 and 2 is 12, and 3 times 12 is 36. Then the difference between 36 − 4 = 32.

75. The correct answer is (A). The pattern in this series is made by adding +1, +4, +1, +4, and so on.

76. The correct answer is (C). The difference between 34 and 6 is 28. Now 28 divided by 4 is 7.

77. The correct answer is (D). Determine the amounts for (P), (Q), and (R). Here, (P) = 18, (Q) = 18, and (R) = 42. When you test each alternative to see which is correct, you see that choice (D) is the correct answer: (R) is greater than (P).

78. The correct answer is (B). Let x be the number, then 4 times of x is $4x$, and 1/4th time of $4x$ is x, hence $x = 40$.

79. The correct answer is (B). The circumference of the circle = πd unit, where d is the diameter; therefore, circumference = 5π cm.

80. The correct answer is (B). Here x, y, and z all are positive number, so it is obvious that 2(x+y+z) is the largest number.

81. The correct answer is (C). The pattern in this series is made by adding x2, +2, x2, +2, and so on.

82. The correct answer is (B). $4 \times 4 \times 4 \times 4 \times 4 = 1024$, is the largest number, so (Q) is the largest number.

83. The correct answer is (B). 60 divided by 2 = 30 and 30 divided by 5 is equal to 6.

84. The correct answer is (C). Here $\frac{2x}{10} = \frac{16}{20}$, then $x = 4$.

85. The correct answer is (B). The number of elements of A = 7.

86. The correct answer is (B). S = t (5 + 6) – (11–2t), where t = 1, then S = 11 – 9 = 2.

87. The correct answer is (C). $\angle ACD = 140°$, $\angle BAC = 90°$, so $\angle ACB = 180° - 140° = 40°$. Therefore, $\angle ABD = 180° - 90° - 40° = 50°$.

88. The correct answer is (C). 30% of 400 = 400 × 0.3 = 120.

89. The correct answer is (B). $0.06 > \frac{1}{36}$.

90. The correct answer is (D). 0.3742 rounded to nearest hundredth is 0.37.

91. The correct answer is (B). 8 quarts = 2 gallons. Therefore, 8 quarts is the largest value.

92. The correct answer is (D). It is obviously that 09 > 0.87.

93. The correct answer is (C). The pattern in this series is made by adding 4 to each number.

94. The correct answer is (D). Here 36 and 49 are relatively prime to each other, so the greatest common factor of 36 and 49 is 1.

95. The correct answer is (C). Here we can observe that (R) is larger than (S).

96. The correct answer is (C). Solution for x : 2x + 5 = 17, then 2x = 12 so x = 6.

97. The correct answer is (D). Let x be the number, then $x \times \frac{12}{100} = 30$. Then $x = 250$.

98. The correct answer is (D). Here it is obvious that 27 > 72.

99. The correct answer is (B). 12% of 200 is = 200 × 0.12 = 24.

100. The correct answer is (B). The pattern in this series is made by adding 4 to each number.

101. The correct answer is (B). Here the linear operation:

$$2 + (6 \times 4) \div 8$$

$$= 2 + 24 \div 8$$

$$= 2 + 3$$

$$= 5$$

102. The correct answer is (A). The pattern in this series is made by adding +1, +4, +1, +4, and so on.

103. The correct answer is (C). $1 = 100c. Therefore, 100 : 70 = 10 : 7.

104. The correct answer is (B). 16 divided by 4 is 4, and 6 times 4 is equal to 24.

105. The correct answer is (D). The natural numbers are 1, 2, and 3. Therefore, there are 3 natural numbers.

106. The correct answer is (C). The decimal representation of $\frac{9}{10} = 0.9$.

107. The correct answer is (D). The solution of $(-5)2\ 5 = 25 \times 5 = 125$.

108. The correct answer is (B). The solution for y: x + 4y = 21, where x = 1, then 4y = 20, hence y = 5.

109. The correct answer is (A). The cube of 8 = 8 × 8 × 8 = 512, dividing 512 by 4 we will get 128.

110. The correct answer is (D). 10% of 810 = 810 × 0.1 = 81, 4 less of 81 = 77.

111. The correct answer is (D). The pattern in this series is made by adding 2 to each number.

112. The correct answer is (C). The number is (8 + 7) × 5 = 15 × 5 = 75.

Reading Comprehension Skills

113. The correct answer is (A). The narrative is by the author sharing her memories of love for her father.

114. The correct answer is (B). The narrative is by the author sharing her memories of love for her father.

115. The correct answer is (C). A girdle is a thing that surrounds something like a belt or girdle. It talks about how the author needs support to stop herself from sad thoughts.

116. The correct answer is (D). The author focused her narrative on how she misses the newspaper hats her father made despite the unpleasant experience she had when she was younger.

117. The correct answer is (A). See sentence 9.

118. The correct answer is (A). The narrative is by the author sharing her memories of love for her father, remembering their good old times making newspaper hats.

119. The correct answer is (C). C'mere is (informal) for come here.

120. The correct answer is (D). The author was remembering her father. Reminiscence involves sharing thoughts and feelings of one's experiences to recall and reflect upon important events within one's life.

121. The correct answer is (B). See title.

122. The correct answer is (C). Paragraph 4 is when the author started recalling events from the past with her father.

123. The correct answer is (B). See title.

124. The correct answer is (A). See sentence 1. At kindergarten, she was asked by a classmate, "Why did you kill Jesus?" which she did not understand.

125. The correct answer is (C). A pilgrimage is a pilgrim's journey to a shrine or a sacred place.

126. The correct answer is (A). Spouting off is to spout words in a way that is hasty, irresponsible.

127. The correct answer is (C). Longing is a strong desire especially for something unattainable: craving.

128. The correct answer is (D). To tuck away is to keep something out sight.

129. The correct answer is (D). The prefix fore means before. Forewarning is an advance warning.

130. The correct answer is (B). Heathen means relating to heathens; pagan. A person who does not belong to a widely held religion (especially one who is not a Christian, Jew, or Muslim) as regarded by those who do.

131. The correct answer is (B). The whole story talked about her awakening of how different their beliefs are from her classmates, neighbor, and to her grandparents.

132. The correct answer is (A). Ripple means to utter or play with a slight rise and fall of sound.

133. The correct answer is (A). It's easy to read the essay as it is, but in between the lines you will understand that the prince, being a male and the main character, was glamorized as described by the rippling effect of the way he speaks regardless of what he said. "Of course, I have a mistress," the prince rippled.

134. The correct answer is (B). Tool can also be a verb which means drive, ride.

135. The correct answer is (C). Buttoned-down is widely referred to as a garment but also means formal and old-fashioned or boring. In this essay, the speaker expresses her distaste with racism and how the white boys were given too much attention compared to her ancestors back then.

136. The correct answer is (D). The essay talked about how racism affects how each individual's worth is valued.

137. The correct answer is (A). To chatter is to click repeatedly or uncontrollably (due to cold).

138. The correct answer is (C). Drastic means extreme in effect or action: severe.

139. The correct answer is (B). "Has been exploring" is the complete verb used in the sentence in the present perfect progressive tense indicating that the action has started and is continuous.

140. The correct answer is (C). "Has been exploring" is the complete verb used in the sentence in the present perfect progressive tense indicating that the action has started and is continuous. You form the present perfect progressive by using have been (or has been) followed by an – *ing* verb.

141. The correct answer is (B). See sentence 3.

142. The correct answer is (A). See title.

143. The correct answer is (D). See sentence 1 under directions.

144. The correct answer is (A). While preheating the oven, you can do the other steps in the recipe. Preheating your oven can help make sure you're cooking food to the correct temperature.

145. The correct answer is (B). Unprecedented means not known or experienced before; not normal.

146. The correct answer is (C). Unrelenting means not yielding in strength, severity, or determination; unstoppable.

147. The correct answer is (C). Being resilient means being able to withstand or recover quickly from difficult conditions.

148. The correct answer is (A). Urban refers to or in, relating to, or characteristic of a town or city.

149. The correct answer is (A). Stoking means to make greater in size, amount, or number; add coal or other solid fuel to.

150. The correct answer is (B). Inhabited also means developed, cultivated, or occupied.

151. The correct answer is (C). See paragraph 2, sentence 8.

152. The correct answer is (D). See paragraph 2, sentence 9.

Vocabulary

153. The correct answer is (A). Antipathy is a deep-seated feeling of dislike, aversion.

154. The correct answer is (C). To call someone austere is to see them as stern and cold in appearance or manner.

155. The correct answer is (B). Clout is an informal word for influence or power.

156. The correct answer is (D). Culmination is the highest or climactic point of something, especially as attained after a long time.

157. The correct answer is (D). Deference means respect and esteem due a superior or an elder, in consideration of.

158. The correct answer is (B). Demur is the action or process of objecting to or hesitating over something.

159. The correct answer is (C). To deplete is to use up the supply or resources of; diminish in number or quantity.

160. The correct answer is (D). Dire means extremely serious or urgent.

161. The correct answer is (A). To disparage is to regard or represent as being of little worth.

162. The correct answer is (D). Egregious means outstandingly bad; shocking.

163. The correct answer is (B). To be eloquent means to be fluent or persuasive in speaking or writing.

164. The correct answer is (B). Entrenched means (of an attitude, habit, or belief) firmly established and difficult or unlikely to change; ingrained.

165. The correct answer is (A). Erratic means not even or regular in pattern or movement; unpredictable.

166. The correct answer is (C). To expend is spend or use up (a resource such as money, time, or energy).

167. The correct answer is (D). To foment is to instigate or stir up (an undesirable or violent sentiment or course of action).

168. The correct answer is (B). Galvanize means to shock or excite (someone) into taking action.

169. The correct answer is (D). Ignominious means deserving or causing public disgrace or shame.

170. The correct answer is (A). To incite is to encourage or stir up (violent or unlawful behavior).

171. The correct answer is (A). To abjure is to renounce upon oath.

172. The correct answer is (A). Bellicose means demonstrating aggression and willingness to fight.

173. The correct answer is (C). Deleterious means causing harm or damage.

174. The correct answer is (B). Fatuous means silly and pointless.

Mathematics Concepts

175. The correct answer is (C). 1 year = 12 months, then the ratio of 7 months and 12 months = 7 : 12.

176. The correct answer is (A). 162 = 256 and 172 = 289, here 259 < 286 < 289.

177. The correct answer is (C). It is obvious that 4 > 0.4.

178. The correct answer is (A). The factorization of 48 = 2 × 2 × 2 × 2 × 3.

179. The correct answer is (D). The commutative property is $a \cdot b = b \cdot a$.

180. The correct answer is (B). The intersection is {1, 4, 5, 7, 9} ∩ {1, 3, 9, 12} = {1, 9}.

181. The correct answer is (C). The subtraction between $12 - 3\frac{2}{3} = 8 + \frac{1}{3} = 8\frac{1}{3}$.

182. The correct answer is (B). Mr. Wilson paid $624.36 for insurance policy for last year, then he paid in one month = $\$\frac{720}{12} = \$60$.

183. The correct answer is (B). The solution is equal to = 4 + (−20) + 6 + (−12) = −16 − 6 = −22.

184. The correct answer is (B). Let x be the price of the Xerox machine, then 10% of x = $180, then $0.1x = 80$, so $x = 1800$, therefore the price of the computer with tax is = $1,800. Then the price of the computer without tax = $(1800 – 180) = $1,620.

185. The correct answer is (B). The addition of $3\frac{7}{9} + 7\frac{2}{9} = 10 + \frac{9}{9} = 10 + 1 = 11$.

186. The correct answer is (C). Solution for x: 4x = 24, then x = 6.

187. The correct answer is (D). Let x be the principal amount, then S.I. = $\frac{P \times R \times T}{100}$; therefore P = $\frac{100I}{R \times T}$; therefore P = $1,400.

188. The correct answer is (D). Here A = 7, B = 5, then 3A + 4B = 3 × 7 + 4 × 5 = 41.

189. The correct answer is (B). The solution for x: 5(7x – 8) = 30, 7x = 14; therefore x = 2.

190. The correct answer is (B). The subtraction of $2\frac{2}{3} + 1\frac{4}{3} = 1 - \frac{2}{3} = \frac{1}{3}$.

191. The correct answer is (D). The area of the rectangle = 5 ft. x 4 ft. = 20 sq. ft.

192. The correct answer is (C). The ratio between $\frac{10}{13}$ and $\frac{5}{4}$ is $\frac{10}{13} : \frac{5}{4}$, i.e., 8 : 13.

193. The correct answer is (A). The division = $\frac{4.278}{8.46} = 0.5056 \,(\text{Approx.})$.

194. The correct answer is (A). Given that A = 4, B = 6, and C = 5, then $\frac{5B}{AC} = \frac{5.6}{4.5} = \frac{3}{2}$.

195. The correct answer is (D). The solution for x: 6x = 48 × 5, then x = 40.

196. The correct answer is (A). The volume of the solid = 6 × 4 × 10 cc = 240 cc

197. The correct answer is (B). The multiplication of 64 × 927 = 59,328.

198. The correct answer is (C). The percentage of 4 over 20 is ($\frac{4}{20} \times 100$)% = 20%.

199. The correct answer is (A). The solution for x: 4x = 36, then x = 9.

200. The correct answer is (C). The 10 factors of 48 are: 1, 2, 3, 4, 6, 8, 12, 16, 24, 48. The 8 factors of 56 are: 1, 2, 4, 7, 8, 14, 28, 56. The greatest common factor of 48 and 56 is 8.

201. The correct answer is (C). The product of 5 and 3 is 15 and the sum of 5 and 3 is 8, then the difference between 15 and 8 is 7.

202. The correct answer is (D). The solution: 4 × 2 = 8 and 12/3 = 4, then 8/4 = 2.

203. The correct answer is (C). ab + 56 = 92, where a = 6, then b = $\dfrac{36}{6}$ = 6.

204. The correct answer is (C). The area of the square is = 52 = 25 cm².

205. The correct answer is (D). The solution for x: x = $\dfrac{224}{7}$ = 32.

206. The correct answer is (C). The solution for x: Here x2 + 9 = 73, then x2 = 64 hence, x = ± 8.

207. The correct answer is (B). The surface area = 6 a2 sq. unit = 6 × 7 × 7 sq. cm = 294 sq. cm.

208. The correct answer is (B). $\angle BAC = 40°$, $\angle ACD = 120°$, so $\angle ACB = 180° - 120° = 60°$. Therefore, $\angle ABC = 180° - 100° = 80°$.

209. The correct answer is (C). The division of $56 \div \dfrac{1}{7} = 8$.

210. The correct answer is (B). 50% of 80 is 40, and 5 more of 40 is 45.

211. The correct answer is (C). The solution for x: Here 4x + 3 > 3x + 4, then 4x – 3x > 4 – 3, therefore x > 1.

212. The correct answer is (B). The solution for x: Here 5x + 13 = 58, 5x = 45, then x = 9.

213. The correct answer is (C). The addition of 0.902 + 5.9 + 5.26 = 12.062.

214. The correct answer is (B). The solution x: $x^2 + 9 = 25$, then x = 4.

215. The correct answer is (B). (8 + 9)2 = 289.

216. The correct answer is (C). The perimeter of a square = 4 × a cm = 4 × 4 = 16 cm.

217. The correct answer is (D). The solution for r where n = 1, r = 36 – 7 = 29.

218. The correct answer is (B). The radius of the circle = 4/2 cm = 2 cm.

219. The correct answer is (A). Solving for y, given equations 2x + 4y = 10 and x + y = 2, then solving for y we get y = 3 by multiplying 2nd equation with 2 and subtract both equations we get y = 3.

220. The correct answer is (B). The number increased by 140%, then the number is 40 × 140% = 40 × 1.4 = 56.

221. The correct answer is (D). The cube root of 5832 = 18.

222. The correct answer is (B). From 8:40 a.m. to 14:40 Elena was not at her home, and then she was not at home for 6 hours long.

223. The correct answer is (A). The solution for x: $4.5x + 6.5 = 15.5$. Then $x = 2$.

224. The correct answer is (B). Let x be the number, then $x + 38 = 64$, so $x = 26$.

225. The correct answer is (B). Let x be the number, then 50% of $x = \dfrac{5x}{10}$, therefore $\dfrac{5x}{10} = 16$, so $x = \dfrac{16 \times 10}{5} = 32$.

226. The correct answer is (C). The solution for y: $6x - 2y = 4$, at $x = 2$, $6 \times 2 - 2y = 4$, then $12 - 4 = 2y$, hence, $y = 4$.

227. The correct answer is (A). The solution for s: $s = t(10 + 5) - (10 - t)$ at $t = 2$, then $s = 30 - 8 = 22$.

228. The correct answer is (B). 25 times 25 = 625.

229. The correct answer is (C). 18 times 5 = 90, then 90 + 12 = 102.

230. The correct answer is (D). 400% of 80 = 4 times 80 = 320.

231. The correct answer is (B). The correct statement is 7 feet > 2 feet.

232. The correct answer is (A). The pattern in this series is +3, +3, +3, +3, and so on. So the next number will be 13 + 3 = 16.

233. The correct answer is (A). The multiplication of $9 \times 9 \times 9 = 729$.

234. The correct answer is (C). The solution for y: when $x = 3$ and $y = 7 + 8x$, so, $y = 7 + 24 = 31$.

235. The correct answer is (B). The circumference of the circle is $= \pi d = \pi \times 10$ cm. $= 10\pi$ cm.

236. The correct answer is (B). $20^2 = 400$ and $21^2 = 441$. Then 419 is between 20 and 21.

237. The correct answer is (A). Solving for x: $7x - 5x = 11 - 7$, then $x = 2$.

238. The correct answer is (C). The sum of 18 + 13 + 7 + 24 + 8 = 70. The average $70 \div 5 = 14$.

Language

239. The correct answer is (B). New York City is the only city being referred to because it is described as the largest. There can only be one largest. Notice that the determiner "the" is used before "United States" because it is a group of states.

240. The correct answer is (A). Adam does not need a determiner "the" because he is the first man and there should only be one.

241. The correct answer is (C). "Their" is a pronoun of ownership.

242. The correct answer is (D). The word "there" has multiple functions. In verbal and written English, the word can be used as an adverb, a pronoun, a noun, an interjection, or an adjective. This word is classified as an adverb if it is used to modify a verb in the sentence.

243. The correct answer is (A). "They're" is a contraction of they are.

244. The correct answer is (C). "Your" is a pronoun of ownership. "You're" is a contraction of "you are".

245. The correct answer is (B). "You're" is a contraction of "you are".

246. The correct answer is (D). Whether means in any case.

247. The correct answer is (A). "Weather" is the state of the atmosphere with respect to heat or cold, wetness or dryness, calm or storm, clearness or cloudiness.

248. The correct answer is (B). "Really" is an adverb describing the extent of how fast she talked.

249. The correct answer is (C). "Quickly" is an adverb describing the manner he stood. You cannot use "quicker" when there is no comparison.

250. The correct answer is (A). "You" is plural pronoun therefore have should be the proper verb to use. When using the past tense "did," the base form of the verb must be used.

251. The correct answer is (D). The action is present perfect progressive. There is no indication when the action had stopped, which is why letter B is not the correct answer.

252. The correct answer is (B). The action is past perfect progressive. There is an indication that the action had stopped when the rain poured.

253. The correct answer is (C). The action is future perfect progressive. To form a future perfect progressive, the verb "will have been" must be accompanied by the base form of the verb followed by the time of the action in the future.

254. The correct answer is (A). "About" has multiple purposes. It can be used as a preposition, an adverb, or an adjective. In this statement, letter A correctly used <u>about</u> as a preposition.

255. The correct answer is (A). Letter A used "at" as a preposition correctly. It is used to specify the time and place.

256. The correct answer is (D). The correct preposition is "in" because the cake must be inside the oven to be baked.

257. The correct answer is (B). The correct preposition is "on" indicating that the sweets are placed on the surface of the countertop.

258. The correct answer is (B). The usage of the word "with" is as a preposition. It is used to indicate associations, togetherness, and connections between things and people. Letter B correctly used "with".

259. The correct answer is (A). As Susan is generally a female name and she is the subject of the second sentence, the correct pronoun is "she".

260. The correct answer is (C). Birthday is a name of an event, noun.

261. The correct answer is (A). "On birthdays" is an adverb of time indicating when you get gifts.

262. The correct answer is (B). Running in the sentence is used as a subject, noun.

263. The correct answer is (B). Running is an action word in the sentence.

264. The correct answer is (C). Happy in the sentence is an adjective describing the quality of thoughts.

265. The correct answer is (B). "Happily" is an adverb describing the manner he/she will be thinking.

266. The correct answer is (B). Sixty-eight is the count of the balloons which modifies the noun, adjective.

267. The correct answer is (A). One-fourth in the sentence is the subject, noun.

268. The correct answer is (B). One-fourth in the sentence modifies the noun, sheet of paper, therefore it is an adjective.

269. The correct answer is (A). "Violets" is the name of the flower mentioned in the sentence, noun.

270. The correct answer is (C). Violet in the sentence modifies the noun, her eyes, therefore it is an adjective.

271. The correct answer is (D). Stream in the sentence is used as a verb, an action done by the tears on her face.

272. The correct answer is (A). Stream in the sentence is a noun. It refers to a small, narrow river.

273. The correct answer is (C). Face is used as a verb in the sentence which also means confront or deal.

274. The correct answer is (B). Face is used as a noun in the sentence which refers to his front image.

275. The correct answer is (A). "Is" is a be verb.

276. The correct answer is (C). "Are" is a be verb.

277. The correct answer is (C). "There" in the sentence is an adverb of place.

278. The correct answer is (D). "Yet" in the sentence is an adverb of time.

Spelling

279. The correct answer is (C). <u>Writing</u> is spelled with one T.

280. The correct answer is (A). Subtle just like the rest of words is pronounced with a silent B.

281. The correct answer is (A). Acquit means to discharge completely (as from an accusation or obligation).

282. The correct answer is (N). Nothing is misspelled. All words are spelled with two consecutive consonants c and q which is pronounced as "k".

283. The correct answer is (B). Absence is a state or condition in which something expected, wanted, or looked for is not present or does not exist.

284. The correct answer is (D). Address is the same spelling both used as a noun or a verb.

285. The correct answer is (A). Argument is the act or process of arguing, reasoning, or discussing; verb is "argue".

286. The correct answer is (B). All the words are spelled with two consecutive vowels I and e.

287. The correct answer is (C). The rest are correctly spelled with double consonants.

288. The correct answer is (C). The rest are correctly spelled with double consonants. Cheetah is spelled with two consecutive "e".

Sentence Composition

289. The correct answer is (B). "Rein" refers to the straps you use to guide a horse. To reign is to rule or command a kingdom.

290. The correct answer is (A). "Supposably" isn't a real word: It's a cross between "presumably" and "supposedly."

291. The correct answer is (B). To ensure is to make certain while to insure refers to buying insurance.

292. The correct answer is (B). Deep-seated means "firmly established" or "ingrained."

293. The correct answer is (A). When you give someone a "piece of your mind," you're letting them know why you're angry.

294. The correct answer is (A). Peak is the tip of the mountain. The correct word is <u>sneak peek,</u> which means a glimpse.

295. The correct answer is (B). "To slight" someone is to insult or snub them, while sleight means deceitful craftiness.

296. The correct answer is (B). A "principle" is a belief, philosophy, or fundamental truth while principal can mean "main," or "major." It can also refer to capital before interest.

297. The correct answer is (B). Adverse is something leading to harmful effects while "averse" means strongly opposed to.

298. The correct answer is (A). To appraise is to determine the value of an item while to apprise is to inform.

HSPT Report

There are 3 types of scores on the HSPT report:

Raw Score

The student receives a point for every correct answer, and there are no penalties for incorrect or omitted answers.

Standard Score

Standard scores are raw scores that have been converted to a standardized scale so they can be statistically analyzed. The conversion process accounts for differences in difficulty levels between multiple forms of the test so that scores are consistent and comparable across forms.

Each subtest and composite score have their own standard score scale. Standard score scales range from 200 to 800, with a mean of 500 and standard deviation of 100.

Standard scores represent equal units of measurement across a continuous scale and are invariant from year to year and edition to edition. Consequently, the standard score scale is an absolute, unchanging frame of reference which permits group comparisons to be made year after year with precision and confidence. If the standard score in a given subject area is higher than the previous year, growth has occurred.

Percentile Rank

To provide additional meaning to a student's standard score, performance is also reported in terms of a percentile rank. In simplest terms, a percentile rank compares a student's performance on the test to some reference group of students within the same grade level. The percentile rank scale ranges from a low of 1 to a high of 99, with 50 being exactly average.

Percentile ranks do not represent actual amounts of achievement, rather, they compare the relative standing of a student with other students. It is important to know that unlike standard scores, percentile ranks are not on an equal interval scale, meaning they do not represent equal units of measure. For example, the difference between percentile ranks 10 and 20 is not the same difference in achievement as the difference between percentile ranks 60 and 70.

The score report will also offer several other performance analyses, including national and local percentiles, standard scores, grade equivalents, and cognitive skills quotients.

High School
Placement Test 3

Verbal Skills

You have 16 minutes to answer the 60 questions in the Verbal Section.

Directions:

Choose the best answer for each question.

---

1. Which among the words below does not belong?

   (A) Few   (B) Little   (C) Each   (D) Another

2. Which among the words below does not belong?

   (A) Few   (B) Anyone   (C) Many   (D) Both

3. Which among the words below does not belong?

   (A) All   (B) Several   (C) None   (D) Some

4. Which among the words below does not belong?

   (A) Either   (B) Neither   (C) Others   (D) Less

5. Which among the words below does not belong?

   (A) He   (B) She   (C) One   (D) They

6. Which among the words below does not belong?

   (A) She   (B) Her   (C) Hers   (D) They

7. Which among the words below does not belong?

   (A) Him   (B) Them   (C) Their   (D) They

8. Which among the words below does not belong?

   (A) United Kingdom   (B) Country   (C) Vacation   (D) Empire

9. Which among the words below does not belong?

   (A) Karen   (B) Lady   (C) Millie   (D) Erika

10. Which among the words below does not belong?

    (A) Sand   (B) Cement   (C) Dust   (D) Streetlights

11. Which among the words below does not belong?

    (A) Cars   (B) Trucks   (C) Busses   (D) Smoke

12. Which among the words below does not belong?

    (A) Talk   (B) Is talking   (C) Has been talking   (D) Talked

13. Which among the words below does not belong?

    (A) Has read   (B) Reads   (C) Read   (D) Will read

14. Which among the words below does not belong?

    (A) Saw   (B) Had seen   (C) Sees   (D) Had been seeing

15. Which among the words below does not belong?

    (A) Will go   (B) Gone   (C) Will be going   (D) Will have gone

16. Which among the words below does not belong?

    (A) On   (B) Over   (C) Above   (D) Below

17. Which among the words below does not belong?

    (A) Below   (B) Over   (C) Under   (D) Beneath

18. Which among the words below does not belong?

    (A) In   (B) Beside   (C) Next to   (D) By

19. Which among the words below does not belong?

    (A) Almost   (B) Tiny   (C) Always   (D) Often

20. Which among the words below does not belong?

    (A) Never   (B) Seldom   (C) Always   (D) Rarely

21. A pair of eyeglasses is to eyes as braces are to

    (A) Teeth   (B) Ears   (C) Mouth   (D) Nose

22. Pearl is to sphere as box is to

    (A) Cube (B) Cardboard (C) Brown (D) Square

23. Turnip is to vegetable as peach is to

    (A) Sweet (B) Ripe (C) Canned (D) Fruit

24. Quite is to adverb as quiet is to

    (A) Silent (B) Adjective (C) Noisy (D) Preposition

25. Book is to author as editorial is to

    (A) Newspaper (B) Column (C) Editor (D) News

26. Doctor is to medicine as professor is to

    (A) Education (B) University (C) Math (D) Knowledge

27. Rainy is to sunny as cloudy is to

    (A) Sky (B) Bright (C) White (D) Weather

28. Winter is to season as windy is to

    (A) Stormy (B) Weather (C) Breezy (D) Typhoon

29. Floral is to pattern as pink is to

    (A) Feminine (B) Blue (C) Color (D) Girl

30. Sitting is to stool as dining is to

    (A) Eating (B) Food (C) Restaurant (D) Table

31. Which of the following is synonymous with forsake?

    (A) Abandon (B) Accompany (C) Join (D) Together

32. Which of the following is synonymous with accuse?

    (A) Absolve (B) Clear (C) Blame (D) Defend

33. Which of the following is synonymous with adequate?

    (A) Little (B) Less (C) Sufficient (D) Scarce

34. Which of the following is synonymous with hostile?

    (A) Peaceful (B) Aggressive (C) Meek (D) Humble

35. Which of the following is synonymous with tweak?

    (A) Preserve (B) Maintain (C) Protect (D) Alter

36. Which of the following is synonymous with beguile?

    (A) Captivate (B) Bore (C) Repel (D) Avoid

37. Which of the following is synonymous with resentment?

    (A) Indignation (B) Contentment (C) Happiness (D) Satisfaction

38. Which of the following is synonymous with plead?

    (A) Agree (B) Appeal (C) Surrender (D) Concur

39. Which of the following is synonymous with revere?

    (A) Despise (B) Hate (C) Neglect (D) Cherish

40. Which of the following is synonymous with synthetic?

    (A) Artificial (B) Natural (C) Genuine (D) Legitimate

41. Which of the following closely sounds the same as matte?

    (A) Mutt (B) Met (C) Mat (D) Mate

42. Which of the following closely sounds the same as flare?

    (A) Flair (B) Flee (C) Fear (D) Flay

43. Which of the following closely sounds the same as gait?

    (A) Get (B) Gate (C) Gut (D) Gite

44. Which of the following closely sounds the same as wholly?

    (A) Whole (B) Hole (C) Hall (D) Holy

45. Which of the following closely sounds the same as idle?

    (A) Isle (B) Idol (C) Dill (D) Dull

46. Which of the following closely sounds the same as bawled?

    (A) Bold (B) Bode (C) Bald (D) Ball

47. Which of the following closely sounds the same as banned?

    (A) Band (B) Bend (C) Bed (D) Bad

48. Which of the following closely sounds the same as assent?

    (A) Asset (B) Accent (C) Scent (D) Ascent

49. Which of the following closely sounds the same as boulder?

    (A) Builder (B) Bolder (C) Balder (D) Baller

50. Which of the following closely sounds the same as censor?

    (A) Sensor (B) Cursor (C) Seizure (D) Censure

51. Sam went to the movies more often than Kelley. Annie went to the movies more often than Sam. Annie went to the movies more often than Kelley. If the first two statements are true, then the third sentence is

    (A) True (B) False (C) Uncertain

52. Cindy eats more cake than Carol. Carol eats more cake than Ken. Ken eats more cake than Cindy. If the first two statements are true, then the third sentence is

    (A) True (B) False (C) Uncertain

53. Kim's basket weighed less than Rue's. Rose's basket weighed less than Ruby's, Ruby's basket weighed less than Kim's. If the first two statements are true, then the third is

    (A) True (B) False (C) Uncertain

54. Which among the words below does not belong?

    (A) Blue: sky (B) Yellow: sun (C) Pink: blue (D) Red: lips

55. Which among the words below does not belong?

    (A) Diver: ocean (B) Teacher: education (C) Doctor: medicine (D) Lawyer: law

56. Which among the words below does not belong?

    (A) Diver: ocean (B) Teacher: student (C) Teacher: school (D) Nurse: hospital

57. Which among the words below does not belong?

(A) Pen: write   (B) Pencil: draw   (C) Eraser: erase   (D) Notebook: paper

58. Which among the words below does not belong?

(A) Notebook: paper   (B) Bag: cloth   (C) Desk: wood   (D) Notebook: note

59. What are words that sound the same but have different meanings and have different spellings called?

(A) Homophones   (B) Homographs   (C) Homogeneous   (D) Homophobe

60. What are words that are spelled the same but have different meanings called?

(A) Homophones   (B) Homogeneous   (C) Homographs   (D) Homophobe

End of section.

If you have any time left, go over the questions in this section only.

Do not start the next section.

You have 30 minutes to answer the 52 questions in the Quantitative Skills Section.

Directions:

Choose one answer—the answer you think is best—for each problem.

---

61. What is the average of 6 + 14 + 29 + 1 + 15?

(A) 46   (B) 65   (C) 13   (D) 17

62. Look at the series: 24, 27, 30, _____, 36. What will be the number to fill the blanks?

(A) 31   (B) 34   (C) 35   (D) 33

63. $6^2 + 8^2 =$

(A) 13^2 (B) 12^2 (C) 11^2 (D) 10^2

64. Solve for y : 2x + 3y = 10, where x = 2

(A) y = 2   (B) y = 3   (C) y = 4   (D) y = 5

65. Simplify: $(-4)^2(6)$

(A) 16   (B) –16   (C) 96   (D) –96

66. As a decimal $\frac{7}{8}$ is

(A) 0.587   (B) 0.875   (C) 0.785   (D) 0.885

67. What number is cube of 6 divided by 4?

(A) 216   (B) 54   (C) 45   (D) 36

68. Look at the image:

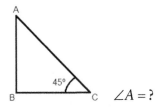

$\angle A = ?$

(A) 90^0 (B) 60^0 (C) 45^0 (D) 180^0

69. What will be 5 less, 20% of 80?

    (A) 16   (B) 21   (C) 11   (D) 12

70. Solve the operation:
    $4 + (7 \times 4) \div 14$

    (A) 4   (B) 2   (C) 6   (D) 8

71. Look at the series 6, 8, 9, 11, 12, 14, ___. What number should come next?

    (A) 16   (B) 15   (C) 12   (D) 17

72. The ratio of 40¢ and 50¢ is

    (A) 8 : 9   (B) 9 : 5   (C) 4 : 5   (D) 5 : 6

73. What number is 7 times $\dfrac{1}{5}$ of 40?

    (A) 40   (B) 35   (C) 56   (D) 50

74. How many natural numbers are between 2 and 5?

    (A) 2   (B) 3   (C) 4   (D) 5

75. Find the ratio between 5 day and 2 weeks.

    (A) 5 : 2   (B) 5 : 12   (C) 5 : 10   (D) 5 : 14

76. The square root of 125 is between

    (A) 10 to 11   (B) 11 to 12   (C) 12 to 13   (D) 13 to 14

77. Which one of the following is true?

    (A) 30 < 3.0   (B) –10 < –4   (C) 4 < 0.4   (D) 91 > 122

78. The prime fraction of 78 is

    (A) $2 \times 3 \times 16$ (B) $2 \times 3 \times 13$ (C) $2 \times 3 \times 6 \times 8$ (D) $2 \times 3 \times 5 \times 8$

79. Find the perimeter of a square whose side is 9 cm.

    (A) 81 cm   (B) 18 cm   (C) 36 cm   (D) 27 cm

80. Increase by 80%, the number 50 becomes

    (A) 40   (B) 50   (C) 80   (D) 90

81. Solve: x + y = 7, x − y = 1, then x =

(A) 7   (B) 4   (C) 3   (D) 5

82. Solve $4x + 9 > 2x + 13$.

(A) $x > 2$ (B) $x < 2$ (C) $x > 4$ (D) $x < 4$

83. Solve: 0.904 + 92 + 5.27 =

(A) 91.874   (B) 98.714   (C) 98.174   (D) None of these

84. $(2 + 4)^2 =$

(A) 16   (B) 4   (C) 20   (D) 36

85. Solve: y + 5x = 20, Find y where x = 2

(A) 10   (B) 15   (C) 20   (D) 25

86. $\sqrt{x-7} = 18$, x =

(A) 9   (B) 5   (C) 8   (D) 4

87. What is 5 more than 40% of 40?

(A) 16   (B) 21   (C) 25   (D) 29

88. Look at the series 32, 35, 38, ____. What number should come next?

(A) 40   (B) 42   (C) 41   (D) 43

89. What will be 4 less 10% of 900?

(A) 90   (B) 86   (C) 94   (D) 82

90. What number is square of 8 divided by 4?

(A) 16   (B) 32   (C) 64   (D) 8

91. Solve the operation,

$4 \times (34 - 9) \div 5$

(A) 5   (B) 4   (C) 20   (D) 25

92. {A, P, E, X} ∩ {M, O, B, I, L, E}

(A) {A, P}   (B) {E, X}   (C) {E}   (D) {X}

93. What is the reciprocal of 4?

(A) $\frac{1}{2}$ (B) $\frac{1}{4}$ (C) $\frac{1}{8}$ (D) $\frac{1}{16}$

94. The circumference of circle is

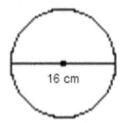

16 cm

(A) 8π cm   (B) 16π cm   (C) 32π cm   (D) π cm

95. The ratio of 50¢ and 80¢ is

(A) $5:8$ (B) $6:7$ (C) $10:17$ (D) $8:5$

96. How many natural numbers are between 51 to 59?

(A) 9   (B) 8   (C) 7   (D) 6

97. Find x

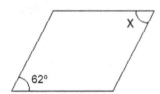

x

62°

(A) $x = 62^0$ (B) $x = 38^0$ (C) $x = 28^0$ (D) $x = 52^0$

98. What is 2 greater than $\frac{5}{6}$ of 12?

(A) 10   (B) 12   (C) 8   (D) 6

99. Look at the series and find the next number: 2, 5, 8, 11, ____.

(A) 13   (B) 14   (C) 12   (D) 15

100. What number is 5 times $\frac{1}{5}$ of 30?

(A) 5   (B) 6   (C) 30   (D) 25

101. What number is 30 more than $\frac{5}{7}$ of 49?

    (A) 5 (B) 35 (C) 30 (D) 65

102. What number is 6 more than 5 squared?

    (A) 25 (B) 19 (C) 31 (D) 29

103. Look at the series: 10, 15, 20, 25, ____. What number will be the next number?

    (A) 25 (B) 30 (C) 35 (D) 40

104. Which angle is obtuse angle?

    (A) 89^0 (B) 49^0 (C) 180^0 (D) 174^0

105. Solve: 62.92 × 0.0736

    (A) 4.630912 (B) 4.360192 (C) 4.036192 (D) 3.046192

106. Solve: $4x - 9 = 5x - 11$, $x =$

    (A) $x = 1$ (B) $x = 2$ (C) $x = 3$ (D) $x = 4$

107. If A% of 60 of 15, A =

    (A) A = 25 (B) A = 20 (C) A = 30 (D) A = 40

108. The greatest common factor of 10, 25 is

    (A) 10 (B) 5 (C) 0 (D) 1

109. Solve: 72, 592 × 180

    (A) 13,055,202 (B) 13,085,200 (C) 13,055,220 (D) 13,220,055

110. Solve: 9 × 3 ÷ (6 ÷ 2)

    (A) 9 (B) 6 (C) 3 (D) 12

111. Solve: $x^2 + 9 = 58$

    (A) $x = \pm6$ (B) $x = \pm7$ (C) $x = \pm8$ (D) $x = \pm9$

112. $\dfrac{9x}{4} + 3 = 30$, $x =$

    (A) $x = 4$ (B) $x = 3$ (C) $x = 12$ (D) $x = 16$

End of section.

If you have any time left, go over the questions in this section only.

Do not start the next section.

You have 25 minutes to answer the 62 questions in the Reading Comprehension and Vocabulary Sections.

Directions:

Read each passage carefully and choose the best answer for each question.

"The Mysterious Inner Life of The Octopus" by Martha Henriques

It was a big night for Inky the octopus. The day's visitors had been and gone, and now his room in the aquarium was deserted. In a rare oversight, the lid of his tank had been left ajar. The common New Zealand octopus had been without female company for some time, sharing a tank with only a fellow male, Blotchy. The loose lid provided Inky with an opportunity. With eight strong suckered limbs and, quite possibly, intimate concerns on his mind, Inky hauled himself out of the water, made his way under the loose lid, and off across the aquarium floor.

He made it about 13ft (4m) when he found something else—not a mate, but a drain that emptied into the Pacific Ocean. With that, Inky was gone.

(No one, besides Blotchy, was there to witness this great escape. But with the help of a wet trail and a few telling sucker marks, Inky's movements were later pieced together by the staff of the New Zealand National Aquarium in the city of Napier.)

As Inky demonstrated in his famous escapade, octopuses are enterprising animals adept at problem solving. They are acutely intelligent and able to learn novel tasks and orient themselves within their environment. There is also growing consensus that octopuses are most likely sentient.

113. What animal is the topic of the article?

    (A) Octopus (B) Shrimp (C) Sea creature (D) Squid

114. What is the name of the animal which is the main subject of the article?

    (A) Inky (B) Blotchy (C) Napier (D) No name

115. What is the name of the animal the main subject shared a tank with?

    (A) Inky (B) Blotchy (C) Napier (D) Blinky

116. What does the underlined word mean?
    The day's visitors had been and gone, and now his room in the aquarium was <u>deserted</u>.

    (A) Occupied (B) Full (C) Empty (D) Crowded

117. What does the underlined word mean?
    In a rare oversight, the lid of his tank had been left <u>ajar</u>.

    (A) Locked (B) Secured (C) Slightly opened (D) Closed

118. What does the underlined word mean?

Inky <u>hauled</u> himself out of the water, made his way under the loose lid, and off across the aquarium floor.

(A) Stayed put   (B) Sunk lower   (C) Stood still   (D) Pull with difficulty

119. What does the underlined word mean?

But with the help of a wet <u>trail</u> and a few telling sucker marks, Inky's movements were later pieced together.

(A) Appearance   (B) Track   (C) Clothing   (D) Nuts

120. What does the underlined word mean?
Octopuses are <u>enterprising</u> animals adept at problem solving.

(A) Unimaginative   (B) Clueless   (C) Unintelligent   (D) Ingenious

121. What does the underlined word mean?
Octopuses are enterprising animals <u>adept</u> at problem solving.

(A) Mediocre   (B) Proficient   (C) Inept   (D) Amateur

122. What does the underlined word mean?

There is also growing consensus that octopuses are most likely <u>sentient</u>.

(A) Conscious   (B) Unaware   (C) Unconscious   (D) Unknowing

"The Mysterious Inner Life of The Octopus" by Martha Henriques (continuation)

People who work with octopuses or who spend a lot of time in their company describe the sense that when you look at an octopus, there is something looking back.

"When you're dealing with an octopus who's being attentively curious about something, it is very hard to imagine that there's nothing experienced by it," says Peter Godfrey-Smith, professor of history and philosophy of science at the University of Sydney in Australia, and author of Other Minds: The Octopus and the Evolution of Intelligent Life. "It seems kind of irresistible. That itself is not evidence, that's just an impression."

Given this hunch as a starting point, how do you begin to explore the consciousness of an animal so unlike ourselves?

To start with, what do philosophers and scientists mean by "consciousness" in this context? Godfrey-Smith takes it as meaning there is "something it is like to be that animal". In a famous essay, the philosopher Thomas Nagel asks, "What is it like to be a bat?" Nagel described the problem that imagining the inner experience of a bat is very difficult, if not impossible, when your reference point is the human body and your own human mind.

123. Who is the Peter Godfrey-Smith?

(A) Author of *Other Minds: The Octopus and the Evolution of Intelligent Life*   (B) Author of the article "The Mysterious Inner Life of the Octopus"   (C) Philosopher of the famous essay "What Is It Like to Be a Bat?"   (D) Worker at the New Zealand National Aquarium in the city of Napier

124. Who is Thomas Nagel?

(A) Author of *Other Minds: The Octopus and the Evolution of Intelligent Life*   (B) Author of the article "The Mysterious Inner Life of the Octopus"   (C) Philosopher of the famous essay "What Is It Like to Be a Bat?"   (D) Worker at the New Zealand National Aquarium in the city of Napier

125. Who is Martha Henriques?

(A) Author of *Other Minds: The Octopus and the Evolution of Intelligent Life*   (B) Author of the article "The Mysterious Inner Life of the Octopus"   (C) Philosopher of the famous essay "What Is It Like to Be a Bat?"   (D) Worker at the New Zealand National Aquarium in the city of Napier

126. What does the author of *Other Minds: The Octopus and the Evolution of Intelligent Life* have to say about an octopus?

(A) "What is it like to be a bat?"   (B) "When you're dealing with an octopus who's being attentively curious about something, it is very hard to imagine that there's nothing experienced by it."   (C) That imagining the inner experience of a bat is very difficult, if not impossible   (D) Describe the sense that when you look at an octopus, there is something looking back

127. What does the philosopher have to say in his famous essay about bats?

(A) "What is it like to be a bat?"   (B) "When you're dealing with an octopus who's being attentively curious about something, it is very hard to imagine that there's nothing experienced by it."   (C) That imagining the inner experience of a bat is very difficult, if not impossible   (D) Describe the sense that when you look at an octopus, there is something looking back

128. What does the underlined word mean?

People who work with octopuses or who spend a lot of time in their <u>company</u>.

(A) A commercial business   (B) An establishment   (C) An institution   (D) Presence

129. What does the underlined word mean?

"When you're dealing with an octopus who's being <u>attentively</u> curious about something, it is very hard to imagine that there's nothing experienced by it."

(A) Not showing interest at all   (B) Distracted by another thought   (C) Not mentally present

(D) Paying close attention

130. What does the underlined word mean?

"It seems kind of <u>irresistible</u>."

(A) Inviting   (B) Unappealing   (C) Ugly   (D) Boring

131. What does the underlined word mean?

Given this <u>hunch</u> as a starting point, how do you begin to explore the consciousness of an animal so unlike ourselves?

(A) Impression   (B) Fact   (C) Truth   (D) Reality

132. What does the underlined word mean?

Nagel described the problem that imagining the inner experience of a bat is very difficult, if not <u>impossible</u>.

(A) Easy   (B) Unfeasible   (C) Unattainable   (D) Bearable

"The Mysterious Inner Life of The Octopus" by Martha Henriques (continuation)

Likewise, imagining an octopus's inner life is a hard thing to do from our human standpoint. Try it for a moment—imagine what it's like to be suspended in the cool blueish twilight down at the seabed, perhaps a slight drag of current pulling you this way and that, your eight arms waving gently around you. When you picture the tips of your suckered limbs moving, what do you imagine it feels like? Is it, perhaps, something like wiggling your human fingers and toes?

Now add into the equation that an octopus is an invertebrate, with no skeleton at all. Its legs have no femur, tibia or fibula, no feet, and no toes to wiggle. Instead, octopuses have a hydrostatic skeleton, combining muscular contraction and water's resistance to compression to generate movement. This is very different from your own experience of moving your extremities—a little closer might be when we move our tongues, which also make use of hydrostatic pressure. Indeed, the octopus's limbs are covered in suckers that have unique sensors that taste everything they touch.

"The octopus's arms are, in some ways, more like lips or tongues than hands," says Godfrey-Smith. "There's a whole great cascade of sensory information of that taste-based form that's coming in every time the animal does anything. That's very different from our situation."

133. What does the underlined word mean?

Likewise, imagining an octopus's inner life is a hard thing to do from our human <u>standpoint</u>.

(A) Place where someone is standing   (B) Pointed stand   (C) Perspective

(D) Standing while pointing

134. What does the underlined word mean?

—imagine what it's like to be suspended in the cool blueish <u>twilight</u> down at the seabed

(A) Dawn   (B) Daybreak   (C) Nightfall   (D) Vampire

135. What does the underlined word mean?

Now add into the equation that an octopus is an <u>invertebrate</u>.

(A) Lacking a backbone   (B) Inside out   (C) Capable of vibrating   (D) Inverted

136. What does the underlined word mean?

This is very different from your own experience of moving your <u>extremities</u>.

(A) Starting point   (B) Beginning   (C) Inner   (D) Limbs

137. What does the underlined word mean?

Indeed, the octopus's limbs are covered in suckers that have unique <u>sensors</u> that taste everything they touch.

(A) Dummy   (B) Receptor   (C) Scale   (D) Diagram

138. What does the underlined word mean?

"There's a whole great <u>cascade</u> of sensory information of that taste-based form that's coming in every time the animal does anything".

(A) Tiny   (B) Outpouring   (C) Unnoticed   (D) Slight

139. Which among the words below is similar in meaning to the underlined word?

<u>Likewise</u>, imagining an octopus's inner life is a hard thing to do from our human standpoint.

(A) In addition   (B) On the other hand   (C) But   (D) However

"The Mysterious Inner Life of The Octopus" by Martha Henriques (continuation)

Take a closer look at the octopus's nervous system, and things get even stranger. The octopus's arms have more autonomy than our human arms and legs do. Each has its own miniature brain, giving it a degree of independence from the animal's central brain. Our own nervous system, however, is highly centralised, with the brain the seat of sensory integration, emotion, initiating movement, behaviour and other actions.

"One of the real challenges we have is to try to work out what experience might be like in a less centralised, less integrated kind of system," says Godfrey-Smith. "In the case of the octopus, people sometimes ask whether there might be multiple selves present. I think it's just one self per octopus, but there might be a kind of partial fragmentation, or just a sort of looseness there."

The closer you look at the octopus's body and nervous system, the harder it becomes to grasp—or believe you are grasping—what it might be like to be an octopus. After all, the last common ancestor we shared with octopuses lived 600 million years ago (an uninspiring-looking animal something like a flatworm).

140. What was the difference between humans and octopus's nervous system cited on the article?

(A) The human nervous system is highly centralized compared to an octopus which has arms that have more autonomy than human extremities   (B) The octopus' nervous system is highly centralized compared to a human whose has arms have more autonomy than octopus' extremities   (C) The human nervous system is highly dispersed compared to an octopus which has arms that have more autonomy than human extremities   (D) The octopus' nervous system is highly dispersed compared to a human whose has arms have more autonomy than octopus' extremities

141. What does the underlined word mean?

Our own nervous system, however, is highly <u>centralised</u>, with the brain the seat of sensory integration, emotion, initiating movement, behaviour and other actions.

(A) Dispersed   (B) Scattered   (C) Devolved   (D) Unified

142. What was the last common ancestor we shared with the octopuses?

(A) Squid   (B) Jelly fish   (C) Something like a flatworm   (D) 600 million years ago

143. How long ago did the last common ancestor we shared with octopuses lived?

(A) Squid   (B) 600 million years ago   (C) Something like a flatworm   (D) 900 million years ago

"The Mysterious Inner Life of The Octopus" by Martha Henriques (continuation)

Take, for instance, the ability to feel pain—the focus of the LSE team's report on cephalopod molluscs (which include octopuses, cuttlefish and squid) and decapod crustaceans (which include crabs, crayfish, lobsters, prawns and shrimps). Browning and her colleagues reviewed more than 300 scientific papers to distil eight criteria that suggest an animal can feel pain:

1. possession of nociceptors (receptors that detect noxious stimuli—such as temperatures hot enough to burn, or a cut)
2. possession of parts of the brain that integrate sensory information
3. connections between nociceptors and those integrative brain regions
4. responses affected by local anaesthetics or analgesics
5. motivational trade-offs that show a balancing of threat against opportunity for reward
6. flexible self-protective behaviours in response to injury and threat
7. associative learning that goes beyond habituation and sensitisation
8. behaviour that shows the animal values local anaesthetics or analgesics when injured

An animal can meet a criterion with a high, medium or low level of confidence, depending on how conclusive or inconclusive the research is. If an animal meets seven or more of the criteria, Browning and her colleagues argue there is "very strong" evidence that the animal is sentient. If it meets five or more with a high level of confidence, there is "strong evidence" of sentience, and so on.

Using this measure, Browning and her colleagues concluded that there was little doubt octopuses could feel pain, and were therefore sentient. They met all but one of the criteria with high or very high confidence, and one with medium confidence. They scored most highly out of the creatures studied—more so even than their cousin the cuttlefish, who are considered to be more intelligent. (Browning notes, though, that far less research has been done on cuttlefish and other cephalopods besides octopuses, which affects their scores.)

The report was used as evidence to inform an amendment to the UK's Animal Welfare (Sentience) Bill to recognize that cephalopod mollusks and decapod crustaceans are sentient.

"I think that's a good thing, the fact that in the UK octopuses and also crustaceans are getting a new kind of recognition in animal rights," says Godfrey-Smith.

The ability to feel pain is just one of the many facets of consciousness—there is also the ability to feel pleasure, to feel bored or interested, to experience companionship, and many more. With more research, scientists may be able to devise similar scales to measure more of these different aspects of consciousness in animals.

144. What does the underlined word mean?

Browning and her colleagues reviewed more than 300 scientific papers to distil eight criteria that suggest an animal can feel pain.

(A) Impair (B) Extract (C) Install (D) Implant

145. What does the underlined word mean?

motivational trade-offs that show a balancing of threat against opportunity for reward

(A) Argument (B) Debate (C) Misunderstanding (D) Compromise

146. What does the underlined word mean?

An animal can meet a criterion with a high, medium or low level of confidence, depending on how conclusive or inconclusive the research is.

(A) Convincing (B) Unconvincing (C) Unbelievable (D) Doubtful

147. What does the underlined word mean?

The report was used as evidence to inform an amendment to the UK's Animal Welfare (Sentience) Bill to recognize that cephalopod mollusks and decapod crustaceans are sentient.

(A) Destruction (B) Original (C) Authentic (D) Correction

148. What does the underlined word mean?

The ability to feel pain is just one of the many facets of consciousness.

(A) Flat surface (B) A tap where water runs (C) Face to face (D) A feature

149. How can one ascertain that animal can feel pain according to the article?

(A) Using the measure of level of confidence among the nine criteria distilled from Browning and her colleagues' research (B) Using the measure of level of confidence among the six criteria distilled from Browning and her colleagues' research (C) Using the measure of level of confidence among the eight criteria distilled from Browning and her colleagues' research (D) Using the measure of level of confidence among the seven criteria distilled from Browning and her colleagues' research

150. How many levels of confidence are there on the measure researchers use to prove that animals can feel pain?

(A) Three: high, medium, low   (B) Two: high, low   (C) Two: present, absent

(D) Three: complete, incomplete, partial

151. How many criteria does an animal need to meet to conclude that there is "very strong" evidence that the animal is sentient?

(A) If an animal meets three or more of the criteria; or five or more with a low level of confidence, there is "very strong" evidence that the animal can feel pain   (B) If an animal meets seven or more of the criteria; or five or more with a high level of confidence, there is "very strong" evidence that the animal can feel pain   (C) If an animal meets seven or more of the criteria; or five or more with a medium level of confidence, there is "very strong" evidence that the animal can feel pain   (D) If an animal meets seven or more of the criteria; or five or more with a low level of confidence, there is "very strong" evidence that the animal can feel pain

152. What does the research say about octopuses?

(A) That there was little doubt that octopuses can feel pain   (B) That there was little doubt that octopuses cannot feel pain   (C) That for sure octopuses cannot feel pain   (D) The research did not prove anything

Vocabulary

Directions:
Choose the word that closely means the same as the underlined word.

153. Extra caution is <u>advised</u>

(A) Recommended the best course of action   (B) Allowed independence to choose

(C) Provided options   (D) Absolute law

154. Heed to the elder's <u>advice</u>

(A) Guidance offered   (B) Command from a superior   (C) Enforced by law   (D) A demand from

155. <u>Heed</u> to the elder's advice

(A) Disregard   (B) Ignore   (C) Overlook   (D) Follow

156. The king <u>absolved</u> the pirates of their crimes.

(A) Incarcerate   (B) Pardon   (C) Blamed   (D) Condemned

157. The teacher has given <u>ample</u> time to complete the assignments before the term ends.

(A) Insufficient (B) Limited (C) Meager (D) Adequate

158. As <u>meek</u> as a lamb

(A) Wild (B) Proud (C) Impatient (D) Gentle

159. <u>Ensnared</u> in the city traffic

(A) Trapped (B) Released (C) Free (D) Out

160. To <u>woo</u> his beloved Laura

(A) Leave (B) Push away (C) Court (D) Give up

161. <u>Beseeched</u> to be left behind

(A) Allow (B) Implored (C) Let go (D) Freed

162. <u>Mesmerized</u> by the siren's beauty

(A) Rid (B) Avoid (C) Neglected (D) Charmed

163. Continued to <u>assert</u> his innocence

(A) Declare confidently (B) Mumbled through (C) Whispered (D) Stuttered

164. The <u>burden</u> of being the eldest sibling

(A) Something burning (B) A heavy load (C) A happy circumstance (D) A positive aftermath

165. With the help of his <u>colleagues</u>

(A) An institution where college students go (B) A union of employees (C) A person you work with

(D) An icon

166. Rewarded a <u>considerable</u> amount

(A) Tiny (B) Unacceptable (C) Limited (D) Hefty

167. Opted for a <u>conventional</u> wedding

(A) Traditional (B) Unusual (C) Modern (D) Radical

168. <u>Crucial</u> for survival

(A) Unnecessary (B) Significant (C) Minor (D) Unimportant

169. <u>Deficit</u> from today's sale

(A) More than the expected   (B) Shortfall   (C) Surplus   (D) Profit

170. <u>Depict</u> a life of content

(A) Portray   (B) Not characterize   (C) Lack   (D) Fail

171. <u>Devote</u> herself to science

(A) Veer away   (B) Steer clear of   (C) Dedicate   (D) Keep away from

172. <u>Dominate</u> the business world

(A) Govern   (B) Follow   (C) Be a servant   (D) Exit

173. An <u>elite</u> school for royalty

(A) Normal   (B) Local   (C) Public   (D) Superior

174. <u>Expose</u> their family's secret

(A) Hide   (B) Lock away   (C) Secure   (D) Reveal

End of section.

If you have any time left, go over the questions in this section only.

Do not start the next section.

You have 45 minutes to answer the 64 questions in the Mathematics Concepts Section.

Directions:

Choose one answer—the answer you think is best—for each problem. You may use scratch paper when working on these problems.

175. The prime fraction of 28 is

(A) 2.2.14 (B) 2.2.7 (C) 2.7.14 (D) 2.5.14

176. Solve: $2.5x + 7.5 = 10$, $x =$

(A) $x = 2$ (B) $x = 1$ (C) $x = 3$ (D) $x = 4$

177. Solve: $0.72 + 0.92$

(A) 1.46 (B) 1.64 (C) 1.66 (D) 1.44

178. $\angle ABC =$

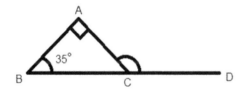

(A) 115^0 (B) 105^0 (C) 125^0 (D) 135^0

179. Find the area of triangle whose dimensions are $h = 16$ inch., $b = 8$ inch.

(A) 128 sq. inch. (B) 64 sq. inch. (C) 32 sq. inch. (D) 16 sq. inch.

180. Solve: $72 \div \dfrac{1}{8}$

(A) 9 (B) 8 (C) 72 (D) 12

181. What number divided by 4, less 9 more than 6?

(A) 60 (B) 15 (C) 20 (D) 30

182. If, $7 + 4x = 23$, $x =$

(A) 4   (B) 16   (C) 32   (D) 12

183. Solve: $3\frac{2}{3} + 4\frac{1}{3}$

(A) $7\frac{2}{3}$ (B) $7\frac{1}{3}$ (C) 7   (D) 8

184. Solve: $12 - 2\frac{2}{5}$

(A) $10\frac{2}{5}$ (B) $9\frac{3}{5}$ (C) $10\frac{3}{5}$ (D) $10\frac{4}{5}$

185. Solve: $7 + (-12) + 22 + (-10)$

(A) 10   (B) 7   (C) 8   (D) 6

186. Look at the series: 6, 8, 10, 12, 14, 16, ____. What number should come next?

(A) 18   (B) 17   (C) 15   (D) 20

187. If A = 5, B = 3, then 3A + 4B =

(A) 12   (B) 15   (C) 3   (D) 27

188. $5(2x - 4) = 40$, $x =$

(A) 12   (B) 6   (C) 8   (D) 10

189. $\{2, 4, 5, 7, 9\} \cap \{1, 4, 3, 9\}$ is equal to

(A) ϕ (B) $\{2, 4, 3\}$ (C) $\{4, 9\}$ (D) $\{2, 4, 5, 7, 9\}$

190. $(3 + 9)^2 =$

(A) 9   (B) 12   (C) 144   (D) 81

191. 40 is 25% of what number?

(A) 40   (B) 80   (C) 60   (D) 160

192. 16% of 200 =

(A) 32   (B) 44   (C) 16   (D) 8

193. Look at the series: 2, 6, 11, 15, 20, ____. What number shall come next?

(A) 25   (B) 24   (C) 26   (D) 28

194. Solve: $2x + 9 = 15$

(A) $x = 3$ (B) $x = 4$ (C) $x = 5$ (D) $x = 6$

195. $\dfrac{7x}{5} = 49$, then $x =$

(A) 5   (B) 7   (C) 35   (D) 49

196. Solve: $64 \times 900 =$

(A) 56,700   (B) 57,600   (C) 55,700   (D) 58,600

197. $5x - 7 = 12x - 49$, $x =$

(A) 35   (B) 5   (C) 42   (D) 6

198. $y = 27 - (4 + 3)\, x$, where $x = 2$, $y =$

(A) 13   (B) 27   (C) 14   (D) 41

199. Which of the following is true?

(A) $40 > 30$ (B) $4 > 5$ (C) $0.4 > 0.5$ (D) $-0.04 < -0.05$

200. $a + b = 3$, $a - b = 1$, then $b =$

(A) $b = 2$ (B) $b = 3$ (C) $b = 1$ (D) $b = 4$

201. Solve: $\dfrac{5.27}{27}$

(A) 0.1952   (B) 0.2951   (C) 0.5912   (D) 0.9512

202. If $A = 5$, $B = 4$, $C = 2$, find $\dfrac{5B}{4C}$

(A) 4   (B) 2   (C) 8   (D) 10

203. Which symbol belongs in the box?

$0.56 \; \square \; \dfrac{5}{6}$

(A) $<$ (B) $>$ (C) $=$ (D) $\geq$

204. Look at the series: 2, 9, 16, ____. What will be the next number?

(A) 20   (B) 22   (C) 23   (D) 24

205. Increased by 110%, the number 80 becomes

(A) 30 (B) 81 (C) 811 (D) 88

206. Find the perimeter of the square whose side is 9 cm

(A) 36 cm (B) 81 cm (C) 18 cm (D) 72 cm

207. p = 27 − (2 + 5) t, where t = 3, p =

(A) 21 (B) 58 (C) 6 (D) 16

208. The reciprocal of 20 is

(A) $\frac{1}{20}$ (B) $\frac{1}{10}$ (C) $\frac{1}{2}$ (D) $\frac{1}{5}$

209. The ratio of 2 days and 1 week is

(A) 2 : 1 (B) 2 : 5 (C) 2 : 7 (D) 2 : 14

210. The circumference of circle is

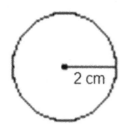

(A) 2π cm (B) 4π cm (C) 8π cm (D) 16π cm

211. If pq + 17 = 54 and q + p, then p =

(A) 27 (B) 9 (C) 3 (D) 18

212. Solve: 2 × 3 ÷ (72 ÷ 12)

(A) 1 (B) 2 (C) 6 (D) 12

213. Find the square root of 289

(A) 15 (B) 17 (C) 19 (D) 13

214. Look at the series: 80, 86, 92, 98, ____. What will be the next number?

(A) 100 (B) 102 (C) 104 (D) 106

215. The greatest common factor of 14, 49 is

(A) 1   (B) 7   (C) 14   (D) 49

216. 12% of 300 =

(A) 12   (B) 24   (C) 36   (D) 48

217. Look at the series: 4, 6, 8, 10, ____. What number should come next?

(A) 10   (B) 12   (C) 14   (D) 19

218. Which is greatest?

(A) 2 weeks   (B) 4 days   (C) 10 days   (D) 12 days

219. Solve for P : 3P + 7 = 19

(A) P = 4   (B) P = 3   (C) P = 2   (D) P = 5

220. What is 0.3459 rounded to nearest tenth?

(A) 0.35   (B) 0.45   (C) 0.34   (D) 0.3

221. Solve: 6 + (–12) + 20 + (–8)

(A) 20   (B) 6   (C) 8   (D) 12

222. Solve: 14 – 3 + 27 + 4

(A) 45   (B) 7   (C) 31   (D) 42

223. Solve for t : 24 – 3t = 6, t =

(A) 6   (B) 9   (C) 10   (D) 12

224. Solve: $2\dfrac{1}{3} - \dfrac{2}{3}$

(A) $1\dfrac{1}{3}$ (B) $1\dfrac{2}{3}$ (C) 2   (D) 3

225. If p = 2, q = 7, then 2p + q =

(A) 7   (B) 9   (C) 11   (D) 10

226. {1, 4, 9} ∩ {2, 4, 6} =

(A) ϕ (B) {4}   (C) {1, 4, 9, 2}   (D) {1, 4, 9, 2, 6}

227. Find the ratio of $\frac{4}{5}$ and $\frac{6}{5}$

(A) $4:5$ (B) $2:3$ (C) $5:6$ (D) $5:4$

228. If $2x + 9 = 4^2 + 1$, then $x =$

(A) 8 (B) 4 (C) 2 (D) 9

229. Solve $4y + 19 = 39$, $y =$

(A) 20 (B) 5 (C) 10 (D) 2

230. The cube root of 324 is

(A) 16 (B) 12 (C) 10 (D) 8

231. What 5% of 200?

(A) 5 (B) 10 (C) 2 (D) 15

232. $\{p, q, r\} - \{p\} =$

(A) $\{p, q, r\}$ (B) $\{p, q\}$ (C) $\{r\}$ (D) ϕ

233. $2x + 4y = 10$, $x + y = 2$, then $y =$

(A) 3 (B) −3 (C) 0 (D) 2

234. $\sqrt{x^2 + 9} = 5$, $x =$

(A) 16 (B) 4 (C) 25 (D) 5

235. Find $\angle x$

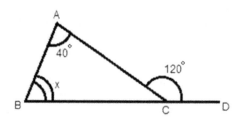

(A) 60^0 (B) 80^0 (C) 100^0 (D) 40^0

236. If $A = 4$, $B = 6$, $C = 5$, then find $\frac{5B}{4C}$.

(A) $\frac{3}{2}$ (B) $\frac{5}{2}$ (C) $\frac{5}{3}$ (D) $\frac{3}{5}$

237. Hope left her home for school at 7:50 a.m., and she came back after school at 1:40 p.m., How long she was not in her home?

(A) 6 Hrs. 50 mins   (B) 4 Hrs. 50 mins   (C) 5 Hrs. 40 mins   (D) 5 Hrs. 50 mins

238. Find the area of the triangle whose dimensions are h = 24 inch., b = 12 inch.

(A) 288 sq. inch   (B) 72 sq. inch   (C) 144 sq. inch   (D) None of these

End of section.

If you have any time left, go over the questions in this section only.

Do not start the next section.

You have 25 minutes to answer the 60 questions in the Language Section.

Directions:

Look for errors in capitalization, punctuation, or usage. Choose the answer with the errors. If no errors found, choose D.

239. (A) The cite is far from the engineer's office.
    (B) The Site is far from the engineers office.
    (C) The site is far from the engineer's office.
    (D) None of the above

240. (A) His belief on hard work has earned him a promotion.
    (B) His believe on hard work has earned him a promotion.
    (C) His belief on hard work has earn him a promotion.
    (D) None of the above

241. (A) Beside the money, she chose to stay because of the benefits.
    (B) Besides the money, she chose to stay because of the benefits.
    (C) Besides the money she chose to stay because of the benefits.
    (D) None of the above

242. (A) The whale belowed a cry.
    (B) The Whale bellowed a cry.
    (C) The whale bellowed a crying.
    (D) None of the above

243. (A) Below the dark sky, I waited for your return.
    (B) Bellow the dark sky, I waited for your return.
    (C) Below the dark sky, me waited for your return.
    (D) None of the above

244. (A) He hurriedly pulled the brake of his car.
    (B) He hurried pulled the brake of his car.
    (C) He hurriedly pulled the break of his car.
    (D) None of above

245. (A) Your saliva break apart the carbohydrates you eat starting the digestion in the mouth.
(B) Your saliva brakes apart the carbohydrates you eat starting the digestion in the mouth.
(C) Your saliva breaks apart the carbohydrates you eat starting the digestion in the mouth.
(D) None of the above

246. (A) It was fathers custom to nap in the afternoon when the sun is blazing hot.
(B) It was father's custom to nap in the afternoon when the sun is blazing hot.
(C) It was father's custome to nap in the afternoon when the sun is blazing hot.
(D) None of the above

247. (A) It is difficult to adapt to the worlds changes.
(B) It is difficult to adopt to the world's changes.
(C) It are difficult to adapt to the world's changes.
(D) None of the above

248. (A) It is better to adopt dogs and cats than to shop.
(B) It is better to adapt dogs and cats than to chop.
(C) It's is better to adopt dogs and cats than to shop.
(D) None of the above

249. (A) Do you believe peer pressure affects your decisions in life?
(B) Do you believe peer pressure affect your decisions in life?
(C) Do you belief peer pressure effects your decisions in life?
(D) None of the above

250. (A) Addiction does not only has negative effects on your body but also your mental and social wellbeing.
(B) Addiction does not only have negative effects on your body but also your mental and social wellbeing.
(C) Addiction does not only have negative affects on your body but also your mental and social wellbeing.
(D) None of the above

251. (A) I'll brought the dress to the tailor to alter it to my size.
(B) I'll bring the dress to the tailor to altar it to my size.
(C) I'll bring the dress to the tailor to alter it to my size.
(D) None of the above

252. (A) The baby's father made faces to amuse her while the mother is away.
(B) The baby's father made faces to bemuse her while the mother is away.
(C) The babies father made faces to amuse her while the mother is away.
(D) None of the above

253. (A) The students were amuse when a different teacher came to class.
     (B) The students were bemused when a different teacher came to class.
     (C) The students was bemused when a different teacher came to class.
     (D) None of the above

254. (A) An royalty exercised absolute power in the olden days.
     (B) The royalty exercised obsolete power in the olden days.
     (C) The royalty exercise absolute power in the olden days.
     (D) None of the above

255. (A) The new teacher's aide is from the seniors.
     (B) The new teacher's aid is from the seniors.
     (C) The new teachers aide is from the seniors.
     (D) None of the above

256. (A) The midwives aid women during childbirth.
     (B) The midwives aide women during childbirth.
     (C) The midwive aid women during childbirth.
     (D) None of the above

257. (A) The chief of the village will welcomed the visitors.
     (B) The chef of the village welcomed the visitors.
     (C) The chief of the village welcomed the visitors.
     (D) None of the above

258. (A) The wealthy families owned states from the countryside.
     (B) The wealthy families owned estates from the countryside.
     (C) The wealthy families' owned estates from the countryside.
     (D) None of the above

259. (A) When water turns into a solid state of matter, it becomes ice.
     (B) When water turns into a solid estate of matter, it becomes ice.
     (C) When water turns into a solid state of matter, it became ice.
     (D) None of the above

260. (A) Water the plants every day.
     (B) Water the plants everyday.
     (C) Watering the plants every day.
     (D) None of the above

261. (A) Loving you is an every day chore that I enjoy.
(B) Loving you is an everyday chore that I enjoy.
(C) Loving you is a everyday chore that I enjoy.
(D) None of the above

262. (A) They laughed at him for chasing after an ellusive dream.
(B) They laughed at him for chasing after an illusive dream.
(C) They laughed at him for chasing after an elusive dreamt.
(D) None of the above

263. (A) She stood out of all the ladies at the ball for her beauty was illusive.
(B) She stood out of all the ladies' at the ball for her beauty was illusive.
(C) She stood out of all the ladies at the ball for her beauty will be illusive.
(D) None of the above

264. (A) It will definitely be an exciting summer.
(B) It will definitively be an exciting summer.
(C) It will definite be an exciting summer.
(D) None of the above

265. (A) The group disassembled the model to inspected each part.
(B) The group dissembled the model to inspect each part.
(C) The group disassembled the model to inspect each part.
(D) None of the above

266. (A) The farm boy chose to disassemble his true emotions for the young lady.
(B) The farm boy chose to dissemble his true emotions for the young lady.
(C) The farm boy chose to dissemble his true emotions on the young lady.
(D) None of the above

267. (A) Some artists go on hiatus to compose there songs.
(B) Some artists go on hiatus to comprise their songs.
(C) Some artists go on hiatus to compose their songs.
(D) None of the above

268. (A) Our store's giveaways comprise of our bestsellers.
(B) Our store's giveaways compose of our bestsellers.
(C) Hour store's giveaways comprise of our bestsellers.
(D) None of the above

269. (A) My parents say that this is just a faze, and I will get out of it.
(B) My parents say that this is just a phase, and I will get out of it.
(C) My parents say that this is just a face, and I will get out of it.
(D) None of the above

270. (A) The effects of the disease are invidious, and it will be too late to notice.
(B) The effects are insidious of the disease, and it will be too late to notice.
(C) The effects are insidious of the disease, and it will be too late too notice.
(D) None of the above

271. (A) The students find it invidious to assign the work close to end of the term.
(B) The students find it insidious to assign the work close to end of the term.
(C) The students find it invidious to assign the work close too end of the term.
(D) None of the above

272. (A) If you're on a budget, you can make a bed out of palates but still look aesthetic.
(B) If your on a budget, you can make a bed out of pallets but still look aesthetic.
(C) If you're on a budget, you can make a bed out of pallets but still look aesthetic.
(D) None of the above

273. (A) I lost my pallet when I saw the mess in the kitchen.
(B) I loss my palate when I saw the mess in the kitchen.
(C) I lost my palate when I saw the mess in the kitchen.
(D) None of the above

274. (A) Who's done the homework?
(B) Whose done the homework?
(C) Whos done the homework?
(D) None of the above

275. (A) Who's shirt is this?
(B) Whos shirt is this?
(C) Whose shirt is this?
(D) None of the above

276. (A) He's the person whom I plan to share the rest of my life with.
(B) He's the person who I plan to share the rest of my life with.
(C) He's the person whose I plan to share the rest of my life with.
(D) None of the above

277.   (A) Joey is an athlete whom also enjoys academics.
       (B) Joey is an athlete who also enjoys academics.
       (C) Joey is an athlete whose also enjoys academics.
       (D) None of the above

278.   (A) Who's did he report to?
       (B) Who did he report to?
       (C) Whose did he report to?
       (D) None of the above

Spelling

Directions:

Identify which among the words is spelled incorrectly. If nothing is misspelled, write N on your answer sheet.

---

279.   (A) Fatigue
       (B) Banquet
       (C) Oblique
       (D) Liqueur

280.   (A) Evaquee
       (B) Habitue
       (C) League
       (D) Accrue

281.   (A) Puerile
       (B) Masquer
       (C) Masquerade
       (D) Duellers

282.   (A) Rehearsal
       (B) Persue
       (C) Appalling
       (D) Receive

283. (A) Lenght
     (B) Strength
     (C) Through
     (D) Thought

284. (A) Taught
     (B) Compel
     (C) Seperate
     (D) Disease

285. (A) Weather
     (B) Collegue
     (C) Commission
     (D) Committed

286. (A) Perceive
     (B) Occur
     (C) Bizzare
     (D) Rhythm

287. (A) Concious
     (B) Advertisement
     (C) Entrepreneur
     (D) Aggressive

288. (A) Minuscule
     (B) Aquire
     (C) Divide
     (D) Assessment

Sentence Composition

Directions:

Choose the best words to complete the sentences.

---

289. She will not listen to her parent's and will take matters in her own hands.

    (A) Advise (B) Advice (C) Advance (D) Advert

290. Doctors strongly against self-medication if symptoms do not improve after a week.

(A) Advise (B) Advice (C) Advance (D) Advert

291. I extend my for the inconvenience this has caused your family.

(A) Apologize (B) Apologies (C) Apology (D) Application

292. I for my absence.

(A) Apologize (B) Apologies (C) Apology (D) Application

293. The gardener chased the moles as they through the garden.

(A) Burrow (B) Borrow (C) Barrow (D) Barrel

294. The neighbor our lawnmower since they do not have one.

(A) Burrowed (B) Borrowed (C) Barrowed (D) Barreled

295. Unknowingly, she sat the prince.

(A) Besides (B) Beside (C) Aside (D) Asides

296. There is no place to go to the old park.

(A) Besides (B) Beside (C) Aside (D) Asides

297. The caged animal gave out a of rage.

(A) Bellow (B) Below (C) Billow (D) Bylaw

298. He wrote the secret message the uninteresting.

(A) Bellow (B) Below (C) Billow (D) Bylaw

End of section.

If you have any time left, go over the questions in this section only.

ANSWER KEY

1. A	31. A	61. B	91. C	121. B	151. B	181. A	211. C	241. B	271. A
2. B	32. C	62. D	92. C	122. A	152. A	182. A	212. A	242. D	272. C
3. B	33. C	63. D	93. B	123. A	153. A	183. D	213. B	243. A	273. C
4. C	34. B	64. A	94. B	124. C	154. A	184. B	214. C	244. A	274. A
5. C	35. D	65. C	95. A	125. B	155. C	185. B	215. B	245. C	275. C
6. D	36. A	66. B	96. C	126. B	156. B	186. A	216. C	246. B	276. A
7. A	37. A	67. B	97. A	127. C	157. D	187. D	217. B	247. D	277. B
8. A	38. B	68. C	98. C	128. D	158. D	188. B	218. A	248. A	278. D
9. B	39. D	69. C	99. B	129. D	159. A	189. C	219. A	249. A	279. N
10. D	40. A	70. C	100. C	130. A	160. C	190. C	220. D	250. B	280. A
11. D	41. C	71. B	101. D	131. A	161. B	191. D	221. B	251. C	281. D
12. D	42. A	72. C	102. C	132. B	162. D	192. A	222. D	252. A	282. B
13. A	43. B	73. C	103. B	133. C	163. A	193. B	223. A	253. B	283. A
14. C	44. D	74. C	104. D	134. C	164. B	194. A	224. B	254. D	284. C
15. B	45. B	75. D	105. A	135. A	165. C	195. C	225. C	255. A	285. B
16. D	46. C	76. B	106. B	136. D	166. D	196. B	226. D	256. A	286. C
17. B	47. A	77. B	107. A	137. B	167. A	197. D	227. B	257. C	287. A
18. A	48. D	78. B	108. B	138. B	168. B	198. A	228. B	258. B	288. B
19. B	49. B	79. C	109. C	139. A	169. B	199. A	229. B	259. A	289. B
20. C	50. A	80. D	110. A	140. A	170. A	200. C	230. D	260. A	290. A
21. A	51. A	81. B	111. B	141. D	171. C	201. A	231. B	261. B	291. B
22. A	52. B	82. A	112. C	142. C	172. A	202. B	232. B	262. D	292. A
23. D	53. C	83. C	113. A	143. B	173. D	203. A	233. A	263. A	293. A
24. B	54. C	84. D	114. A	144. B	174. D	204. C	234. B	264. A	294. B
25. C	55. A	85. A	115. B	145. D	175. B	205. D	235. B	265. C	295. B
26. A	56. B	86. B	116. C	146. A	176. B	206. A	236. A	266. B	296. A
27. B	57. D	87. B	117. C	147. D	177. B	207. C	237. D	267. C	297. A
28. B	58. D	88. C	118. D	148. D	178. C	208. A	238. C	268. A	298. B
29. C	59. A	89. B	119. B	149. C	179. B	209. C	239. C	269. B	
30. D	60. C	90. A	120. D	150. A	180. A	210. B	240. A	270. B	

NOTE: To calculate Raw score, allocate 1 point for each correct answer and 0 points for each incorrect and unanswered questions.

Number of correct answers = _____ (A)

Number of incorrect or unanswered answers = _____ (B)

Final Raw score = A – B = _____ - _____ = _____

EXPLANATIONS

Verbal Skills

1.   The correct answer is (A). B, C, and D are all singular indefinite pronouns. This means that when used in a sentence their count is always singular and must be paired with a singular form of verb. Example: Each sibling has taken an item from their parents as memorabilia.

2.   The correct answer is (B). A, C, and D are all plural indefinite pronouns. When used in a sentence, their count is always plural and must be paired with the base form of the verb. Unlike personal pronouns (e.g., he, she, they), indefinite pronouns do not refer to a specific person or thing already named. Example: Most girls from our class prefer pink over blue.

3.   The correct answer is (B). A, C, and D are indefinite pronouns that can be either singular or plural depending on the context. B is a plural indefinite pronoun and cannot be used to refer to something singular. Example: (singular) All of the work is done. (plural) All of the assignments are due tomorrow.

4.   The correct answer is (C). A, B, and D are all singular indefinite pronouns. This means that when used in a sentence their count is always singular and must be paired with a singular form of verb. Example: Susie goes into the dark room while others stay at the corridor. (plural)

5.   The correct answer is (C). A, B, and D are all personal pronouns. C is an indefinite pronoun. Unlike personal pronouns (e.g., he, she, they), indefinite pronouns do not refer to a specific person or thing already named. Example: One has to sacrifice something to gain something. (Singular indefinite pronoun)

6.   The correct answer is (D). A, B, and C are all feminine possessive pronouns. "They" is a plural personal pronoun that can refer to any gender. Example: She likes ice cream. (Singular and referring to a female). They like ice cream. (Plural and is gender neutral)

7.   The correct answer is (A). B, C, and D are plural gender-neutral pronouns. "Him" is a personal object pronoun. Traditionally, "he" and "him" can be used as a general pronoun when the gender of the subject is unknown, but they are the masculine forms. Example: If anyone sees a suspicious man, he can call the number on the calling card. (Can be anyone, male or female). David walked out when I told him of the bad news. (Referring to David, male)

8.   The correct answer is (A). B, C, and D are common nouns. Common nouns refer to classes or categories of people, animals, places, and things.

9.   The correct answer is (B). A, C, and D are proper nouns. Proper nouns are the names of specific people, animals, and things. They are written with a capital letter at the start.

10. The correct answer is (D). A, B, and C are uncountable nouns. Uncountable nouns, things are seen as a whole or mass. These are called uncountable nouns, because they cannot be separated or counted; expressions such as a bit of, a piece of, an item of, or words for containers and measures must be used. Example: two bags of cement, a handful of sand.

11. The correct answer is (D). A, B, and C are countable nouns. They are items which can be counted. Example: three cars, two busses, one truck.

12. The correct answer is (D). A, B, and C are verbs in their present tense.

    talk – simple present

    is talking – present continuous

    has been talking – present perfect continuous

13. The correct answer is (A). B, C, and D are verbs in their simple tense.

    reads – simple present

    read – simple present or past

    will read – simple future

14. The correct answer is (C). A, B, and D are verbs in their past tense.

    saw – simple past

    had seen – past perfect

    had been seeing – past perfect continuous

15. The correct answer is (B). A, C, and D are verbs in their future tense.

    will go – simple future

    will be going – future continuous

    will have gone – future perfect tense

16. The correct answer is (D). A, B, and C are prepositions for objects placed on an elevated position or top.
    Sample: cat on the table, birds over your head, stars above the sky

17. The correct answer is (B). A, C, and D are prepositions for objects placed at a lower position/level.
    Sample: below the line, under the table, beneath the floor

18. The correct answer is (A). B, C, and D are prepositions for objects at the side.
    Sample: beside the teacher's desk, next to me, by the river

19. The correct answer is (B). A, C, and D are adverbs. An adverb is a word that modifies (describes) a verb (he sings loudly), an adjective (very tall), another adverb (ended too quickly), or even a whole sentence.
Sample: almost home, always by your side, often forgets

20. The correct answer is (C). A, B, and D are adverbs closely similar in meaning.
Sample: never came back, seldom visits him in prison, rarely comes out

21. The correct answer is (A). This is a sample of object–purpose relationship. A pair of eyeglasses are worn to correct visual impairment while braces are worn to correct teeth alignment.

22. The correct answer is (A). This is sample of object–shape relationship. A pearl is a sphere. It is the three-dimensional shape of a pearl, and cube is the three-dimensional shape of a box.

23. The correct answer is (D). This is a sample of object–category relationship. A turnip is a cruciferous vegetable while a peach is a fruit tree.

24. The correct answer is (B). This is a sample of object–category relationship. Quite is an adverb while quiet is an adjective. Sample: changes quite often, the quiet countryside.

25. The correct answer is (C). This is a sample of object–person relationship. A book is written by an author while an editorial, a newspaper article that gives an opinion on a topical issue, is written by an editor.

26. The correct answer is (A). This is a sample of profession/occupation–field relationship. A doctor is a profession in medicine while a professor is a profession in education.

27. The correct answer is (B). This is a sample of antonym relationship. Sunny is the opposite of a rainy weather while cloudy is the opposite of bright skies.

28. The correct answer is (B). This is a sample of specific–general relationship. Winter is one of the seasons while windy is one of the main types of weather (sunny, cloudy, windy, rainy, and stormy).

29. The correct answer is (C). This is a sample of specific–general relationship. Floral is a pattern type on clothing while pink is a color.

30. The correct answer is (D). This is a sample of object–purpose relationship. A stool is used for sitting while a table is used for dining.

31. The correct answer is (A). To forsake someone/something is to leave them/it behind.

32. The correct answer is (C). To accuse someone is to charge someone with an offense or crime.

33. The correct answer is (C). If something is considered at an adequate amount, it is satisfactory or acceptable in quality or quantity.

34. The correct answer is (B). When someone is hostile, he is ready or likely to attack or confront; characterized by or resulting from aggression.

35. The correct answer is (D). To tweak something is to improve (a mechanism or system) by making fine adjustments/changes to it.

36. The correct answer is (A). To beguile someone is to charm or enchant someone, sometimes in a deceptive way.

37. The correct answer is (A). To feel resentment is to feel bitter indignation at having been treated unfairly.

38. The correct answer is (B). To plead is to present and argue for (a position), especially in court or in another public context.

39. The correct answer is (D). To revere something is to feel deep respect or admiration for something.

40. The correct answer is (A). If something is synthetic, it is made by chemical synthesis, especially to imitate a natural product.

41. The correct answer is (C). Matte is pronounced as /mat/ which means dull and flat, without a shine.

42. The correct answer is (A). Flare is pronounced as /fler/ which means a sudden brief burst of bright flame or light. Flair, which is pronounced the same, is a special or instinctive aptitude or ability for doing something well.

43. The correct answer is (B). Gait is pronounced as /gāt/ which refers to a person's manner of walking.

44. The correct answer is (D). Wholly is pronounced as /'hōl(l)ē/ which also means entirely; fully.

45. The correct answer is (B). Idle is pronounced as /'īdl/ which means not active or in use. Idol on the other hand, which is pronounced the same, is a person or thing that is greatly admired, loved, or revered.

46. The correct answer is (C). Bawled, the past tense of bawl and pronounced as /bôld/, means weep or cry noisily.

47. The correct answer is (A). Banned, the past tense of ban and pronounced as /band/, means officially or legally prohibited.

48. The correct answer is (D). Assent is pronounced as /əˈsent/ which refers to the expression of approval or agreement. Ascent, also pronounced /əˈsent/, refers to an upward slope or path.

49. The correct answer is (B). Boulder is pronounced as /ˈbōldər/ refers to a large rock, typically one that has been worn smooth by erosion.

50. The correct answer is (A). Censor is pronounced as /ˈsensər/ which refers to an official who examines material that is about to be released, such as books, movies, news, and art. A sensor, also pronounced /ˈsensər/, is a device which detects or measures a physical property and records, indicates, or otherwise responds to it.

51. The correct answer is (A). Annie went to the movies more often than both Sam and Kelley.

52. The correct answer is (B). Cindy eats more cake than both Carol and Ken, therefore Ken eats less cake than Cindy.

53. The correct answer is (C). We cannot compare Ruby's basket to Kim's as there is no given statement we can use as the point of comparison.

54. The correct answer is (C). A, B, and D are color–object relationships. Sample: sky is blue, sun appears yellow, lips are red.

55. The correct answer is (A). B, C, and D are profession–field relationships. A is a person: place relationship. The ocean is where a diver dives into.

56. The correct answer is (B). A, C, and D are profession–place relationships. A diver dives in the ocean, a teacher teaches at school, a nurse works at the hospital.

57. The correct answer is (D). A, B, and C are object–purpose relationships. You write with a pen, erase with an eraser, draw with a pencil.

58. The correct answer is (D). A, B, and C are object–material relationships. A notebook is made of paper, a bag is made of cloth, a desk is made of wood.

59. The correct answer is (A). Homophones sound the same but have different meanings and have different spellings too. Sample: Altar/ Alter.

60. The correct answer is (C). Homographs are words that are spelled the same but have different meanings. Understand it with examples. Sample: Bow – to incline/ type of knot.

Quantitative Skills

61. The correct answer is (B). The sum of the numbers = 6 + 14 + 29 + 1 + 15 = 65. Then the average $= \dfrac{65}{5} = 13$.

62. The correct answer is (D). The pattern in this series is made by adding 3 to each number.

63. The correct answer is (D). 62 + 82 = 36 + 64 = 100 = 102.

64. The correct answer is (A). Solve for y : $2x + 3y = 10$, here $x = 2$, then $4 + 3y = 10$, so $y = 2$.

65. The correct answer is (C). $(-4) \times (-4) = 16$, then $16 \times 6 = 96$.

66. The correct answer is (B). Decimal representation of $\dfrac{7}{8}$ is = 0.875.

67. The correct answer is (B). Cube of 6 = 6 × 6 × 6 = 216, divided by 4 = 54.

68. The correct answer is (C). Given that $\angle ABC = 90°$, $\angle BCA = 45°$, so $\angle CAB = 180° - 90° - 40° = 45°$. Therefore $\angle CAB = 45°$.

69. The correct answer is (C). 20% of 80 = 20 × 0.8 =16, 5 less of 16 = 16 − 5 = 11.

70. The correct answer is (C). 4 + 28 / 14 = 4 + 2 = 6.

71. The correct answer is (B). The pattern in this series is made by adding +2, +1, +2, +1, and so on.

72. The correct answer is (C). The ratio 40 : 50 = 4 : 5.

73. The correct answer is (C). 40 ÷ 5 = 8, and 7 times 8 = 56.

74. The correct answer is (C). There are 4 natural numbers between 2 and 5.

75. The correct answer is (D). The ratio of 5 days and 2 weeks = 5 : 14.

76. The correct answer is (B). The square of 11 = 121 and square of 12 = 144, then the square root of 125 is between 11 and 12.

77. The correct answer is (B). Obviously the –10 < –4.

78. The correct answer is (B). The prime factorization of 78 = 2 × 3 × 13.

79. The correct answer is (C). The perimeter of the square 4 × 9 = 36 cm.

80. The correct answer is (D). 180% of 50 = 50 × 1.8 = 90.

81. The correct answer is (B). $x + y = 7$ and $x - y = 1$, then adding both equations we get $2x = 8$, then $x = 4$.

82. The correct answer is (A). $4x + 9 > 2x + 13$, therefore $x > 2$.

83. The correct answer is (C). 0.904 + 92 + 5.27 = 98.174.

84. The correct answer is (D). (2 + 4)2 = 62 = 36.

85. The correct answer is (A). Solve for y : y + 5x = 20, where x = 2, then y + 10 = 20, y = 10.

86. The correct answer is (B). $x2 - 7 = 18$, $x2 = 25$, then $x = 5$.

87. The correct answer is (B). 40% of 40 = 40 × 0.4 = 16, 5 more of 16 = 16 + 5 = 21.

88. The correct answer is (C). The pattern in this series is made by adding 3 to each number.

89. The correct answer is (B). 10% of 900 = 900 × 0.1 = 90, 4 less of 90 = 90 – 4 = 86.

90. The correct answer is (A). Square of 8 = 8 × 8 = 64, 64 divided by 4 = 16.

91. The correct answer is (C). Solution: 4 × 25 ÷ 5 = 4 × 5 = 20.

92. The correct answer is (C). The intersection of two sets = {E}.

93. The correct answer is (B). The reciprocal of $4 = \frac{1}{4}$.

94. The correct answer is (B). The diameter of the circle = 16 cm, then the circumference of the circle = π × 16 cm =16π cm.

95. The correct answer is (A). The ratio is 50 : 80 = 5 : 8.

96. The correct answer is (C). There are 7 natural numbers between 51 and 59.

97. The correct answer is (A). For parallelogram opposite angles are equal hence $\angle x = 62°$.

98. The correct answer is (C). $\dfrac{5}{6}$ of 12 = 5 × 2 = 10, 10 less than 2 is = 10 − 2 = 8.

99. The correct answer is (C). The pattern in this series is made by adding 3 to each number. Therefore, the next number will be = 14.

100. The correct answer is (C). $\dfrac{1}{5}$ of 30 = 6, 5 times 6 is = 30.

101. The correct answer is (D). $\dfrac{5}{7}$ of 49 = 5 × 7 = 35, 30 more than 35 = 30 + 35 = 65.

102. The correct answer is (C). Square of 5 = 5 × 5 = 25 and 6 more 25 = 25 + 6 = 31.

103. The correct answer is (B). The pattern in this series is made by adding 5 to each number. Therefore, the next number will be = 30.

104. The correct answer is (D). The obtuse angle is more than 90° and less than 180°, here 174° is the obvious answer.

105. The correct answer is (A). 62.92 × 0.0736 = 4.630912.

106. The correct answer is (B). Solution for x: $4x − 9 = 5x − 11$, then $x = 2$.

107. The correct answer is (A). A% of 60 = 15. Then $\dfrac{A}{100} \times 60 = 15$, then A = 5 × 5 = 25.

108. The correct answer is (B). The factorization of 10 = 2 × 5, and 25 = 5 × 5, then the greatest common factor = 5.

109. The correct answer is (C). Solution: 72,529 × 180 = 13,055,220.

110. The correct answer is (A). Solution: 9 × 3 ÷ (6 ÷ 2) = 27 ÷ 3 = 9.

111. The correct answer is (B). $x2 + 9 = 58$, then $x2 = 49$, $x = \pm 7$.

112. The correct answer is (C). $\dfrac{9x}{4} + 3 = 30$, then $\dfrac{9x}{4} = 27$, $x = 3 \times 4 = 12$.

Reading Comprehension Skills

113. The correct answer is (A). The narrative is by the author sharing her memories of love for her father.

114. The correct answer is (A). See sentence 1. The article mainly talks about the octopus, Inky. Blotchy is its fellow male octopus which it shared a tank with.

115. The correct answer is (B). See sentence 4. Inky shared a tank with a fellow male octopus named Blotchy.

116. The correct answer is (C). Deserted means empty or abandoned.

117. The correct answer is (C). Ajar means slight opened or unlocked.

118. The correct answer is (D). To haul someone/something is to pull or drag with effort or force.

119. The correct answer is (B). A trail is a mark, or a series of signs or objects left behind by the passage of someone or something.

120. The correct answer is (D). Enterprising is an adjective which means having or showing initiative and resourcefulness. It is synonymous with imaginative, ingenious, and creative.

121. The correct answer is (B). Adept is an adjective which means very skilled or proficient at something. It is synonymous with expert, skillful, and talented.

122. The correct answer is (A). Sentient is an adjective which means able to perceive or feel things. It is synonymous with aware, responsive, and reactive.

123. The correct answer is (A). See sentence 2. "When you're dealing with an octopus who's being attentively curious about something, it is very hard to imagine that there's nothing experienced by it," says Peter Godfrey-Smith, professor of history and philosophy of science at the University of Sydney in Australia, and author of *Other Minds: The Octopus and the Evolution of Intelligent Life*.

124. The correct answer is (C). See sentence 6. In a famous essay, the philosopher Thomas Nagel asks, "What is it like to be a bat?" Nagel described the problem that imagining the inner experience of a bat is very difficult, if not impossible, when your reference point is the human body and your own human mind.

125. The correct answer is (B). See title. "The Mysterious Inner Life of the Octopus" by Martha Henriques.

126. The correct answer is (B). See sentence 2. "When you're dealing with an octopus who's being attentively curious about something, it is very hard to imagine that there's nothing experienced by it," says Peter Godfrey-Smith, professor of history and philosophy of science at the University of Sydney in Australia, and author of *Other Minds: The Octopus and the Evolution of Intelligent Life*.

127. The correct answer is (C). See sentence 6. In a famous essay, the philosopher Thomas Nagel asks, "What is it like to be a bat?" Nagel described the problem that imagining the inner experience of a bat is very difficult, if not impossible, when your reference point is the human body and your own human mind.

128. The correct answer is (D). The word "company" can mean any of the choices given but, on the phrase, company means condition of being with another which in this phrase, the octopus.

129. The correct answer is (D). When someone is attentive, he is paying close attention. Sample: Bea attentively listened to the lecture on galaxies.

130. The correct answer is (A). To be irresistible is to be too attractive and tempting to be resisted.

131. The correct answer is (A). A hunch is a feeling or guess based on intuition rather than known facts.

132. The correct answer is (B). If something is impossible, it is described as not able to occur, exist, or be done. Sample: seemingly impossible task.

133. The correct answer is (C). A standpoint is an attitude to or outlook on issues, typically arising from one's circumstances or beliefs.

134. The correct answer is (C). Twilight is the period of the evening when twilight takes place, between daylight and darkness.

135. The correct answer is (A). An invertebrate is an animal lacking a backbone, such as an arthropod, mollusk, annelid, coelenterate, etc. When used as an adjective to describe a person/thing, it means irresolute; spineless.

136. The correct answer is (D). Extremities refer to your hands and feet.

137. The correct answer is (B). A sensor is a device that responds to a physical stimulus. It also means a sense organ for living things which is a bodily structure that receives a stimulus and is affected in such a manner as to initiate excitation of associated sensory nerve fibers which convey specific impulses to the central nervous system where they are interpreted as corresponding sensations, receptor.

138. The correct answer is (B). A cascade is a large number or amount of something occurring or arriving in rapid succession. Sample: a cascade of employee complaints.

139. The correct answer is (A). Likewise means in the same way; also. Other synonyms are in addition, as well, and moreover.

140. The correct answer is (A). See paragraph 1.

141. The correct answer is (D). Centralized means (of an activity or organization) controlled by a single authority or managed in one place. Centralise is the British spelling of centralize.

142. The correct answer is (C). See paragraph 3, last sentence.

143. The correct answer is (B). See paragraph 3, last sentence.

144. The correct answer is (B). To distil is extract the essential meaning or most important aspects of. Sample: my research notes were distilled into a book.

145. The correct answer is (D). A trade-off is a balance achieved between two desirable but incompatible features, a compromise.

146. The correct answer is (A). Conclusive means (of evidence or argument) serving to prove a case; decisive or convincing.

147. The correct answer is (D). An amendment is a minor change or addition designed to improve a text, piece of legislation, etc.

148. The correct answer is (D). A facet refers to one side of something many-sided, especially of a cut gem. It can also refer to a particular aspect or feature of something.

149. The correct answer is (C). See paragraph 1, sentence 2, and enumeration 1–8.

150. The correct answer is (A). See paragraph 2, sentence 1.

151. The correct answer is (B). See paragraph 2, sentences 2–3.

152. The correct answer is (A). See paragraph 3, sentence 1.

Vocabulary

153. The correct answer is (A). Advise is a verb which means to offer suggestions about the best course of action to someone.

154. The correct answer is (A). Advice is a noun which refers to guidance or recommendations offered regarding prudent future action.

155. The correct answer is (C). To heed is to pay attention to; take notice of. Sample: he should have heeded the warnings.

156. The correct answer is (B). To absolve is to set or declare (someone) free from blame, guilt, or responsibility.

157. The correct answer is (D). Ample also means enough or more than enough; plentiful.

158. The correct answer is (D). Meek means quiet, gentle, and easily imposed on; submissive.

159. The correct answer is (A). To ensnare is to catch in or as in a trap. Sample: Spiders ensnare flies and other insects in their webs.

160. The correct answer is (C). To woo is to seek the favor, support, or custom of. In dating, it means to try to gain the love of (someone), especially with a view to marriage.

161. The correct answer is (B). To beseech means to beg for urgently or anxiously. Sample: beseech the Lord's protection.

162. The correct answer is (D). To be mesmerized means to be hypnotized or to be captivated by someone completely so that they cannot think of anything else.

163. The correct answer is (A). To assert means to state a fact or belief confidently and forcefully.

164. The correct answer is (B). Burden refers to a load, a duty, or misfortune that causes hardship, anxiety, or grief; a nuisance.

165. The correct answer is (C). A colleague is a person with whom one works in a profession or business.

166. The correct answer is (D). Considerable means notably large in size, amount, or extent.

167. The correct answer is (A). Conventional means based on or in accordance with what is generally done or believed; traditional.

168. The correct answer is (B). Crucial means of great importance.

169. The correct answer is (B). Deficit means an excess of expenditure or liabilities over income or assets in a given period. Sample: an annual operating deficit.

170. The correct answer is (A). To depict means to show or represent by a drawing, painting, or other art form.

171. The correct answer is (C). To devote means to give all or a large part of one's time or resources to (a person, activity, or cause).

172. The correct answer is (A). To dominate means to have a commanding influence on; exercise control over.

173. The correct answer is (D). Elite means belonging to the richest, most powerful, best-educated, or best-trained group in a society.

174. The correct answer is (D). To expose is to make (something) visible by uncovering it.

Mathematics Concepts

175. The correct answer is (B). The prime factorization of $28 = 2 \times 2 \times 7$.

176. The correct answer is (B). Solution: $2.5x + 7.5 = 10$, then $2.5x = 2.5$, $x = 1$.

177. The correct answer is (B). Solution: $0.72 + 0.92 = 1.64$.

178. The correct answer is (C). $\angle ABC = 35°$, $\angle BAC = 90°$, so $\angle ACB = 180° - 35° - 90° = 55°$. Therefore, $\angle ABD = 180° - 55° = 125°$.

179. The correct answer is (C). The area of the triangle $= \frac{1}{2} \times base \times height = \frac{1}{2} \times 8 \times 16$ sq. inch $= 64$ sq. inch.

180. The correct answer is (A). Solution $72 \div 8 = 9$.

181. The correct answer is (A). 9 more than $6 = 9 + 6 = 15$ and 15 times $4 = 15 \times 4 = 60$.

182. The correct answer is (A). Solution: $7 + 4x = 23$, then $4x = 16$, $x = 4$.

183. The correct answer is (D). Solution: $3 + 4 = 7$ and $\frac{2}{3} + \frac{1}{3} = 1$, then $7 + 1 = 8$.

184. The correct answer is (B). Solution: $12 - 2\frac{2}{5} = 10 - \frac{2}{5} = 9\frac{3}{5}$.

185. The correct answer is (B). Solution: $7 + (-12) + 22 + (-10) = -5 + 12 = 7$.

186. The correct answer is (A). The pattern in this series is made by adding 2 to each number. Therefore, the next number will be $= 18$.

187. The correct answer is (D). Given A = 5, and B = 3, then $3A + 4B = 3 \times 5 + 4 \times 3 = 15 + 12 = 27$.

188. The correct answer is (B). Solution: $5(2x - 4) = 40$. Then $2x - 4 = 8$, so $2x = 12$, Therefore $x = 6$.

189. The correct answer is (C). The intersection is (The common elements of two sets) = {4, 9}.

190. The correct answer is (C). (3 + 9)2 = 122 = 144.

191. The correct answer is (D). Let x be the number where 25% of x = 40. Then $x = \dfrac{100}{25} \times 40 = 160$.

192. The correct answer is (A). 16% of 200 = 200 × 0.16 = 32.

193. The correct answer is (B). The pattern in this series is made by adding +4, +5, +4, +5, and so on.

194. The correct answer is (A). Solution: $2x + 9 = 15$, then $2x = 6$, therefore $x = 3$.

195. The correct answer is (C). Given, $\dfrac{7x}{5} = 49$, then $x = 7 \times 5 = 35$.

196. The correct answer is (B). Solution: 64 × 900 = 57,600.

197. The correct answer is (D). Solution: $5x - 7 = 12x - 49$, then $7x = 42$. Hence $x = 6$.

198. The correct answer is (A). Given that: r = 27 – (4+3) n, where n = 2, hence r = 27 – 7 × 2 = 13.

199. The correct answer is (A). It is obvious that 40 > 30.

200. The correct answer is (C). Given equations a + b = 3 and a – b = 1, adding two equations we have a = 2, then a + b = 3, so 2 + b = 3, therefore b = 1.

201. The correct answer is (A). Division $\dfrac{5.27}{27} = 0.1952$.

202. The correct answer is (B). Given that A = 5, B = 4, and C = 2, therefore $\dfrac{5B}{AC} = \dfrac{5 \times 4}{5 \times 2} = 2$.

203. The correct answer is (A). It is obvious that $0.56 < \dfrac{5}{6}$.

204. The correct answer is (C). The pattern in this series is made by adding 7 to each number. Therefore, the next number will be = 23.

205. The correct answer is (D). 110% of 80 = 80 × 1.1 = 88.

206. The correct answer is (A). The perimeter of the square = 4 × side = 4 × 9 = 36 cm.

207. The correct answer is (C). Given that P = 27 – (2+5) t where t = 3, then P = 27 – 7 × 3 = 27 – 21 = 6.

208. The correct answer is (A). The reciprocal of 20 is = $\dfrac{1}{20}$.

209. The correct answer is (C). The ratio is = 2 days and 1 weeks = 2 : 7.

210. The correct answer is (B). The circumference of the circle = 2πr, where r = radius of the circle. Then the circumference = 2π × 2 cm = 4π cm.

211. The correct answer is (C). Given that pq + 27 = 54, where q = 9, then 9p + 27 = 54. Hence 9p = 27, so p = 3.

212. The correct answer is (A). Solution: 2 × 3 ÷ (72 ÷ 12) = 6 ÷ 6 = 1.

213. The correct answer is (B). 289 = 17 × 17 = 172. Therefore, the square root of 289 = 17.

214. The correct answer is (C). The pattern in this series is made by adding 6 to each number. Therefore, the next number will be = 104.

215. The correct answer is (B). The factors of 14 = 2 × 7 and 49 = 7 × 7. Then the greatest common factor = 7.

216. The correct answer is (C). 12% of 300 = 300 × 0.12 = 36.

217. The correct answer is (B). The pattern in this series is made by adding 2 to each number. Therefore, the next number will be = 12.

218. The correct answer is (A). 2 weeks = 14 days so the greatest option is 2 weeks.

219. The correct answer is (A). Solution: 3p + 7 = 19, then 3p = 12, hence p = 4.

220. The correct answer is (D). The tenth rounded value of 0.3459 = 0.3.

221. The correct answer is (B). 6 + (–12) + 20 + (–8) = –6 +12 = 6.

222. The correct answer is (D). Solution: 14 – 3 + 27 + 4 = 42.

223. The correct answer is (A). 24 – 3t = 6, then 3t = 18, hence t = 6.

224. The correct answer is (B). The subtraction: $2\dfrac{1}{3} - \dfrac{2}{3} = 1\dfrac{2}{3}$.

225. The correct answer is (C). Given that p = 2 and q = 7, then 2p + q = 2 × 2 + 7 = 11.

226. The correct answer is (D). The union of two sets = {1, 4, 9, 2, 6}.

227. The correct answer is (B). The ratio of $\frac{4}{5}$ and $\frac{6}{5}$ is $\frac{4}{5} : \frac{6}{5} = 2 : 3$.

228. The correct answer is (B). Given that $2x + 9 = 16 + 1$, therefore $2x + 9 = 17$, hence $2x = 8$. Then $x = 4$.

229. The correct answer is (B). $4y + 19 = 39$, then $4y = 20$, hence $y = 5$.

230. The correct answer is (D). $324 = 8 \times 8 \times 8 = 83$. Therefore, the cube root of $324 = 8$.

231. The correct answer is (B). 5% of $200 = 200 \times 0.05 = 10$.

232. The correct answer is (B). The subtraction of two sets = {p,q}.

233. The correct answer is (A). Solving for y, given equations $2x + 4y = 10$ and $x + y = 2$, then solving for y we get $y = 3$ by multiplying 2nd equation with 2 and subtract both equations we get $y = 3$.

234. The correct answer is (B). The solution x: $x^2 + 9 = 25$, then $x = 4$.

235. The correct answer is (B). $\angle BAC = 40°$, $\angle ACD = 120°$, $so \angle ACB = 180° - 120° = 60°$. Therefore, $\angle ABC = 180° - 100° = 80°$.

236. The correct answer is (A). Given that A = 4, B = 6, and C = 5, then $\frac{5B}{AC} = \frac{5.6}{4.5} = \frac{3}{2}$.

237. The correct answer is (D). From 7:50 a.m. to 13:40 Hope was not at her home, and then she was not at home for 5 hours and 50 minutes long.

238. The correct answer is (C). The area of the triangle $= \frac{1}{2} \times b \times h = 144$ sq. inch.

Language

239. The correct answer is (C). The word site means location and is not a proper noun, therefore should not be capitalized. The word engineer must have a possessive's to show that the office belongs to the engineer. Cite is mostly used as a verb which means to quote (a passage, book, or author) as evidence. Cite is also known as short for citation.

240. The correct answer is (A). The word belief means an acceptance that a statement is true or that something exists. Believe is a verb which means to accept something as true. To complete a present perfect tense, the verb "has" must be followed by the past participle of the verb "earn" which is "earned."

241. The correct answer is (B). Besides is a preposition which means in addition to. Beside is a preposition used to refer to a location of something; next to. A comma must be present after the prepositional phrase since it was placed at the beginning of the sentence followed by the main subject and predicate.

242. The correct answer is (D). None of the sentences is grammatically correct. The correct verb should be "bellowed" which means emit a deep loud roar, typically in pain or anger. Whale is a common noun which should not be capitalized if it does not start the sentence. Crying is verb. Although "crying" is in the form of a gerund it is not used as a noun in the sentence.

243. The correct answer is (A). Bellow is a verb which means emit a deep loud roar, typically in pain or anger. Below is a preposition referring to a location which means under. The sentence is in active voice, therefore the word "I" must be used instead of "me."

244. The correct answer is (A). A brake refers to a device for slowing or stopping a moving vehicle. "Hurriedly" is an adverb modifying the verb "pulled."

245. The correct answer is (C). The doer of the action "breaks" is your saliva which is the subject of the sentence. Saliva is singular in count. A brake refers to a device for slowing or stopping a moving vehicle.

246. The correct answer is (B). A custom is a thing that one does habitually. The word father must have a possessive's to show that the custom belongs to the father.

247. The correct answer is (D). None of the sentences is grammatically correct. The correct verb is "adapt" which means become adjusted to new conditions. The word "world" must have a possessive's to show that the changes are of the world. It is the subject and is singular in count.

248. The correct answer is (A). It's is a contraction of it is. The correct verb to use is shop which is less preferred according to the sentence.

249. The correct answer is (A). The correct word to use is "believe," which is a verb. Peer pressure is a singular subject, therefore the verb must be "affects." Effect is a noun; affect is a verb.

250. The correct answer is (B). The verb following "does" must follow the base form of the verb, therefore "have" is the correct verb to use. Effect is a noun; affect is a verb.

251. The correct answer is (C). The correct verb to use is "alter" which means to tailor (clothing) for a better fit or to conform to fashion. Altar refers to the table in a Christian church at which the bread and wine are consecrated in communion services. To complete a simple future tense, "will" must be followed by the base form of the verb "bring."

252. The correct answer is (A). The correct verb is "amuse" which means to cause (someone) to find something funny; entertain. Bemuse means to puzzle, confuse, or bewilder (someone). The word baby must have a possessive's to show that the father belongs to the baby.

253. The correct answer is (B). The correct verb is "bemused" which means to puzzle, confuse, or bewilder (someone). The subject "students" is plural.

254. The correct answer is (D). None of the sentences is grammatically correct. The correct adjective is "absolute" which means (of powers or rights) not subject to any limitation; unconditional. The verb should be past tense "exercised" because the statement refers to an action in the past described by the phrase "in the olden days."

255. The correct answer is (A). The correct word is "aide" which means an assistant to an important person. Aid is a verb which means to help. The word teacher must have a possessive's to show that the aide belongs to the teacher.

256. The correct answer is (A). The correct word is "aid" which means to help. The doer of the action is the subject, midwives.

257. The correct answer is (C). The correct word is "chief" which means a leader or ruler of a people or clan. When using the simple future tense, "will" must be followed by the base form of the verb, welcome.

258. The correct answer is (B). The correct word is "estates" which refers to an extensive area of land in the country, usually with a large house, owned by one person, family, or organization. No apostrophe required as "families" is not a possessive noun.

259. The correct answer is (A). State means a physical condition as regards internal or molecular form or structure. The simple present tense of verb must be used as the action has not occurred yet but may occur.

260. The correct answer is (A). "Every day" is an adverbial phrase that means each day. "Everyday" is an adjective. Sample: Shouting is an everyday activity in the Smith's household. The word "everyday" in the sample is modifying the noun "activity." Letter C is an incomplete sentence or a phrase, so a period should not be placed at the end.

261. The correct answer is (B). "Everyday" is an adjective which means happening or used every day; daily. You use "every day" when you need to modify an action which will require an adverb.

262. The correct answer is (D). The correct adjective is "elusive" which means difficult to find, catch, or achieve. The correct noun to use for the phrase "after an elusive dream" is dream. Dreamt is a verb.

263. The correct answer is (A). Illusive means based on or producing illusion; unreal. The word "ladies" does not need the possessive's and the action of the statement is simple past.

264. The correct answer is (A). Definitely is an adverb which means without doubt (used for emphasis). Definitively means decisively and with authority; conclusively. Sample: medicine not definitively proven effective.

265. The correct answer is (C). Disassemble means to take (something) apart. To dissemble is to conceal one's true motives, feelings, or beliefs.

266. The correct answer is (B). To dissemble is to conceal one's true motives, feelings, or beliefs. The correct preposition for the indirect object "young lady" is "for" as the receiver of the action.

267. The correct answer is (C). To compose means to write or create (a work of art, especially music or poetry). Comprise means consist of; be made up of. The correct pronoun to use is "their" which refers to the artists.

268. The correct answer is (A). Comprise means consist of; be made up of. The correct pronoun is "our" which means belonging to or associated with the speaker and one or more other people previously mentioned or easily identified.

269. The correct answer is (B). Phase refers to a stage in a person's psychological development, especially a period of temporary unhappiness or difficulty during adolescence or a particular stage during childhood. Faze means to disturb or disconcert (someone).

270. The correct answer is (B). Insidious means proceeding in a gradual, subtle way, but with harmful effects. Invidious means (of a comparison or distinction) unfairly discriminating; unjust. The correct adverbial phrase is "too late to" followed the base form of the verb.

271. The correct answer is (A). Invidious means (of a comparison or distinction) unfairly discriminating; unjust. 'Too" is an adverb which means in addition; also.

272. The correct answer is (C). Pallet refers to a portable platform for handling, storing, or moving materials and packages. Palate refers to the sense of taste. The correct pronoun to use is "you" followed by the verb "are". "You're" is the contraction of "you are". "Your" is a pronoun referring to ownership.

273. The correct answer is (C). Palate refers to the sense of taste. Loss is a noun which refers to a person or thing or an amount that is lost. Lost is the past participle of the verb lose which is the action done by the subject.

274. The correct answer is (A). "Who's" is the contraction of who is. To complete the question the correct word to use is "who's". Whose is a pronoun which refers to of whom or which (used to indicate that the following noun belongs to or is associated with the person).

275. The correct answer is (C). "Whose" is a pronoun which refers to of whom or which (used to indicate that the following noun belongs to or is associated with the person). The question is asking for the owner of the shirt.

276. The correct answer is (A). "Who" functions as a subject, while "whom" functions as an object. Use who when the word is performing the action. Use whom when it is receiving the action. The noun "person" is the object of the action "share the rest of my life with".

277. The correct answer is (B). "Who" functions as a subject, while "whom" functions as an object. Use who when the word is performing the action. The doer of the action "also enjoys academics" is the subject, Joey.

278. The correct answer is (D). The correct word to use is "whom" as the receiver of the report. The question as asking to whom he reported to.

Spelling

279. The correct answer is (N). Although liqueur looks misspelled, this word is not to be confused with liquor. Liqueur is a sweet alcoholic after-dinner drink. Sample: absinth, absinthe – strong green liqueur flavored with wormwood and anise.

280. The correct answer is (A). Letter A should be spelled "evacuee" which refers to a person who has been evacuated from a dangerous area. Habitue refers to one who frequents a particular place, especially a place offering a specific pleasurable activity.

281. The correct answer is (D). Letter D should be spelled "duelers" (plural) which refers to a person who fights a duel or duels.

282. The correct answer is (B). Letter B should be spelled "pursue" and is one of the most misspelled English words. To pursue means to follow (someone or something) in order to catch or attack them. There is a word "peruse" which means read (something), typically in a thorough or careful way.

283. The correct answer is (A). Letter A should be spelled "length" which refers to the measurement or extent of something from end to end; the greater of two or the greatest of three dimensions of a body.

284. The correct answer is (C). Letter C should be spelled "separate" which means to cause to move or be apart.

285. The correct answer is (B). Letter B should be spelled "colleague" which refers to a person with whom one works in a profession or business.

286. The correct answer is (C). Letter C should be spelled "bizarre" which means very strange or unusual, especially so as to cause interest or amusement.

287. The correct answer is (A). Letter A should be spelled "conscious" which means aware of and responding to one's surroundings; awake.

288. The correct answer is (B). Letter B should be spelled "acquire" which means buy or obtain (an asset or object) for oneself.

Sentence Composition

289. The correct answer is (B). Advice is a noun which refers to guidance or recommendations offered regarding prudent future action. This sentence is talking about the subject not willing to listen to the advice of her parents.

290. The correct answer is (A). Advise is a verb which means to offer suggestions about the best course of action to someone. The verb "advise" is modified by the adverb strongly and the doer of the action is the subject, doctors.

291. The correct answer is (B). Apologies is the plural form of apology. It is a noun and refers to an act of saying that you are sorry for something wrong you have done. Sample: The vice president has sent his apologies.

292. The correct answer is (A). To apologize is to express regret for something that one has done wrong. The doer of the action is the speaker/subject of the sentence. Sample: I must apologize for disturbing you like this.

293. The correct answer is (A). To burrow is to make a hole or tunnel. The doer of the action are the moles. Sample: moles burrowing away underground.

294. The correct answer is (B). To borrow means to take and use (something that belongs to someone else) with the intention of returning it.

295. The correct answer is (B). Beside means at the side of; next to. It is a preposition. Sample: stood beside him.

296. The correct answer is (A). Besides is a preposition which means compared with. Sample: I have no other family besides my parents.

297. The correct answer is (A). Bellow means a deep roaring shout or sound.

298. The correct answer is (B). Below is a preposition which also means at a lower level or layer than. Sample: a stain just below the pocket.

There are 3 types of scores on the HSPT report:

Raw Score

The student receives a point for every correct answer, and there are no penalties for incorrect or omitted answers.

Standard Score

Standard scores are raw scores that have been converted to a standardized scale so they can be statistically analyzed. The conversion process accounts for differences in difficulty levels between multiple forms of the test so that scores are consistent and comparable across forms.

Each subtest and composite score have their own standard score scale. Standard score scales range from 200 to 800, with a mean of 500 and standard deviation of 100.

Standard scores represent equal units of measurement across a continuous scale and are invariant from year to year and edition to edition. Consequently, the standard score scale is an absolute, unchanging frame of reference which permits group comparisons to be made year after year with precision and confidence. If the standard score in a given subject area is higher than the previous year, growth has occurred.

Percentile Rank

To provide additional meaning to a student's standard score, performance is also reported in terms of a percentile rank. In simplest terms, a percentile rank compares a student's performance on the test to some reference group of students within the same grade level. The percentile rank scale ranges from a low of 1 to a high of 99, with 50 being exactly average.

Percentile ranks do not represent actual amounts of achievement, rather, they compare the relative standing of a student with other students. It is important to know that unlike standard scores, percentile ranks are not on an equal interval scale, meaning they do not represent equal units of measure. For example, the difference between percentile ranks 10 and 20 is not the same difference in achievement as the difference between percentile ranks 60 and 70.

The score report will also offer several other performance analyses, including national and local percentiles, standard scores, grade equivalents, and cognitive skills quotients.

CPSIA information can be obtained
at www.ICGtesting.com
Printed in the USA
JSHW062055050423
39911JS00002B/1

9 781839 989025